SHAKESPEARE

in an hour

BY CHRISTOPHER BAKER

SUSAN C. MOORE, SERIES EDITOR

PLAYWRIGHTS in an hour
know the playwright, love the play

IN AN HOUR BOOKS • HANOVER, NEW HAMPSHIRE • INANHOURBOOKS.COM
AN IMPRINT OF SMITH AND KRAUS PUBLISHERS, INC • SMITHANDKRAUS.COM

With grateful thanks to Carl R. Mueller,
whose fascinating introductions to his translations of the Greek and
German playwrights provided inspiration for this series.

Published by In an Hour Books
an imprint of Smith and Kraus, Inc.
177 Lyme Road, Hanover, NH 03755
inanhourbooks.com SmithandKraus.com

Know the playwright, love the play.

In an Hour, In a Minute, and Theater IQ are registered trademarks of
In an Hour Books.

Front cover design by Dan Mehling, dmehling@gmail.com
Text design by Kate Mueller, Electric Dragon Productions
Book production by Dede Cummings Design, DCDesign@sover.net

ISBN-13: 978-1-936232-04-8
ISBN-10: 1-936232-04-9
Library of Congress Control Number: 2009943210

CONTENTS

Why Playwrights in an Hour?

This new series by Smith and Kraus Publishers titled Playwrights in an Hour has a dual purpose for being; one academic, the other general. For the general reader, this volume, as well as the many others in the series, offers in compact form the information needed for a basic understanding and appreciation of the works of each volume's featured playwright. Which is not to say that there don't exist volumes on end devoted to each playwright under consideration. But inasmuch as few are blessed with enough time to read the splendid scholarship that is available, a brief, highly focused accounting of the playwright's life and work is in order.

The central feature of the series, a thirty- to forty-page essay, integrates the playwright into the context of his or her time and place. And the volumes, though written to high standards of academic integrity, are accessible in style and approach to the general reader as well as to the student, and of course to the theater professional and theatergoer.

These books will serve for the brushing up of one's knowledge of a playwright's career, to the benefit of theater work or theatergoing. The Playwrights in an Hour series represents all periods of Western theater: Aeschylus to Shakespeare to Wedekind to Ibsen to Williams to Beckett, and on to the great contemporary playwrights who continue to offer joy and enlightenment to a grateful world.

Carl R. Mueller
School of Theater, Film and Television
Department of Theater
University of California, Los Angeles

Introduction

Despite William Shakespeare's epic status in the theatrical canon, one gnawing issue still plagues his legacy: the authorship controversy, or the assumption that Shakespeare did not write his own plays. Indeed, virtually each of his contemporaries — from the Earl of Oxford, to the Earl of Derby, to Sir Francis Bacon, to Christopher Marlowe, to Mr. W. H., and even Queen Elizabeth herself — has been proposed as the true author. And not all of the conspiracy theorists were loonies; even Sigmund Freud declared himself an Oxfordian.

The reason? Shakespeare never went to university, like Marlowe and Jonson. He only attended Stratford grammar schools.

Apart from the fact that Stratford grammar schools provided a classical education more rigorous than that provided by most contemporary American universities (the majority of which, by the way, no longer even require a Shakespeare course in their English Departments), it is absurd to argue that you must have a university degree in order to invent Shakespeare's verse, plots, and characters. Yet modern academic snobbery often confuses scholarship with imagination.

Did Mozart have a college education? Did Moliere? Did Michelangelo? Actually, the greatest artists of history have often been instinctual, self-taught geniuses who managed their research without the aid of tutors or textbooks.

Still, the most convincing proof that Shakespeare wrote his own plays is the fact that Ben Jonson said he did. Jonson, who had a very strong classical education, was one of the most envious men in literature. He would therefore have been the first to declare Shakespeare an impostor, had that been true. Instead, in the funeral eulogy appended to Shakespeare's First Folio, the first collection of the Bard's plays, Jonson declared that Shakespeare, whom he loved "this side of idolatry," was "a monument without a tomb," a tribute he offered despite the fact that Shakespeare had "little Latin and less Greek," much less that foolish piece of foolscap, otherwise known diploma.

Another enigmatic fact about Shakespeare is his own identity. It is very hard to distill his personality from his plays, probably because he probably had none, or very little, other than *that* geniality that everybody attributes to him. Characters poured through him, and possessed him, like ghosts around a séance table. We know that Shakespeare rarely, if ever, invented his plots. Instead, he took a borrowed story and thrust characters into it, speaking the most powerful and beautiful language ever uttered. If you look at the original models for Hamlet, Falstaff, Iago, Lear, indeed all of Shakespeare's major characters, most of them seem rather puny. What Shakespeare gives them is the heft, arc, and touch of genius.

We concentrate so much on Shakespeare's language and characters that we sometimes fail to appreciate his philosophy. Inheriting all the prejudices of his time — misogyny, macho values, humours theory, racism, and the contemporary version of intelligent design known as the Elizabethan World Picture — he eventually managed to abandon most of them, and envision a malignant universe. It is the misanthropic universe of Timon and Lear, where ingratitude and self-interest reign. It is the savage universe of Iago and Edmund, red in tooth and claw. And although it exists in parallel with the compassionate world of Rosalind and Desdemona and Prospero, it is also a predatory environment, where "humanity must perforce prey upon each other, like monsters of the deep," as Albany fears toward the end of King Lear (1605–1606). For his understanding of all those contradictory things, and for being the kind of instinctual genius that exalts the human race, Shakespeare will always be, in Jonson's words, "not of an age, but for all time."

Robert Brustein
Founding Director of the Yale and American Repertory Theatres
Distinguishing Scholar in Residence, Suffolk University

Shakespeare

IN A MINUTE

AGE	YEAR	
–	1564	Enter William Shakespeare on April 23 (probably), born in Stratford, England.
1	1565	Arthur Golding translates first four books of Ovid's *Metamorphoses*.
6	1570	Palladio publishes *Four Books on Architecture*.
8	1572	St. Bartholomew's Day Massacre of Protestants in France, English fear Catholic invasion.
12	1576	James Burbage builds first outdoor playhouse.
13	1577	Francis Drake begins voyage around the world.
20	1584	Virginia colonized by Sir Walter Raleigh.
23	1587	Mary Queen of Scots loses her head.
24	1588	English turn back the Spanish armada.
26	1590	Edmund Spenser — *The Faerie Queene, Books 1–3*
27	**1591**	**William Shakespeare — *Two Gentleman of Verona***
28	1592	Thomas Kyd — *The Spanish Tragedy* (world premiere)
29	1593	Christopher Marlowe killed in a tavern brawl.
30	1594	Lord Chamberlain's Men, Shakespeare's troupe, formed.
31	**1595**	**William Shakespeare — *A Midsummer Night's Dream***
32	1596	Galileo invents the thermometer.
34	**1598**	**William Shakespeare — *Henry V***
35	1599	The Globe Theatre opens.
36	1600	The East India Company is founded, beginning British expansion to India.
37	**1601**	**William Shakespeare — *Hamlet***
38	1602	Ben Jonson — *The Poetaster*
39	1603	Elizabeth I dies and James I takes the throne.
40	**1604**	**William Shakespeare — *All's Well That Ends Well***
42	**1606**	**William Shakespeare — *Macbeth***
45	**1609**	**Shakespeare's *Sonnets* are published.**
47	1611	The King James Bible is published,
50	1614	Pocahontas marries John Rolfe.
51	1615	Coffee introduced to Italy from Turkey.
52	**1616**	**Exit William Shakespeare.**

A snapshot of the playwright's world. From historical events to pop-culture and the literary landscape of the time, this brief list catalogues events that directly or indirectly impacted the playwright's writing.

Shakespeare

HIS WORKS

Accurately dating Shakespeare's works or developing a precise order of composition is an impossible task. Publication dates give some clues, but publication was a very different business in Shakespeare's day. Records of performance, topical allusions, and textual similarities all help, but are imperfect. The chronology changes as scholarship changes.

The following is modified from one of the best current chronologies, found in *William Shakespeare: A Textual Companion*, by Stanley Wells and Gary Taylor, with John Jowett and William Montgomery.

PLAYS

The Two Gentleman of Verona	1590–91
The Taming of the Shrew	1590–91
Henry VI, Parts I, II, and III	1591–92
Richard III	1592
Titus Andronicus	1592
The Comedy of Errors	1592–94
Love's Labour's Lost	1594–95
Richard II	1595
Romeo and Juliet	1595
A Midsummer Night's Dream	1595
King John	1596
The Merchant of Venice	1596–97
Henry IV, Parts I and II	1596–98
The Merry Wives of Windsor	1597–98
Much Ado About Nothing	1598
Henry V	1598–99

This section presents a complete list of the playwright's works in chronological order by world premiere date.

POETRY

Onstage with Shakespeare

Introducing Colleagues and
Contemporaries of William Shakespeare

 THEATER

Edward Alleyn, English actor
Francis Beaumont, English playwright
Richard Burbage, English actor
Ben Jonson, English playwright, first unofficial poet laureate
Thomas Kyd, English playwright
Christopher Marlowe, English playwright
Tirso de Molina, Spanish playwright
Thomas Middleton, English playwright

 ARTS

William Byrd, English composer
Michelangelo da Caravaggio, Italian painter
El Greco, Cretan/Spanish sculptor and painter
Claudio Monteverdi, Italian composer
Andrea Palladio, Venetian architect
Claude Poussin, French painter
Rembrandt van Rijn, Dutch painter

POLITICS/MILITARY SCIENCE

 Charles IX, French king from 1560–1574
Elizabeth I, queen of England from 1558–1603
Guy Fawkes, English conspirator

This section lists contemporaries whom the playwright may or may not have known.

Ivan IV "the Terrible," Czar of Russia
James VI of Scotland, then James I of England, from 1603–1625
Mary Queen of Scots, Scottish monarch from 1542–1567,
    executed in England, 1587
Pocahontas, Native-American princess

SCIENCE

Tycho Brahe, astronomer
Giovanni Borelli, Italian physiologist and mathematician
Galileo Galilei, Italian scientist
William Gilbert, English scientist and physician
Johannes Kepler, German astronomer
Richard Hakluyt, English geographer and clergyman
Gerardus Mercator, Flemish geographer and cartographer
Andreas Vesalius, Belgian physician and founder of modern
    anatomy

LITERATURE

Samuel Butler, English satirist
Miguel de Cervantes, Spanish novelist, poet, and playwright
John Donne, English poet
Raphael Holinshed, English author, historian
John Milton, English poet, playwright, and pamphleteer
Michel Eyquem de Montaigne, French essayist
François Rabelais, French author
Edmund Spenser, English poet

RELIGION/PHILOSOPHY

Francis Bacon, English essayist, philosopher, and statesman
Giordano Bruno, Italian philosopher
Edmund Campion, English Jesuit priest, Catholic martyr

John Cottom, American religious leader

René Descartes, French philosopher and scientist

Thomas Hobbes, English philosopher

Pope Pius V, issues bull, *Regnans in Excelsis*, excommunicating Elizabeth I.

St. John of the Cross (Juan de Yepes Alvarez), Spanish mystic and friar

SPORTS

Giacomo DiGrassi, Italian fencing master

Jean Forbet, French tennis master

Henry Lee, Queen Elizabeth's Master of the Ordnance and Champion, responsible for jousting tournaments

Ruy Lopez, Spanish, developed modern method of chess playing

Vencento Saviolo, Italian-born English fencing master

George Silver, English fencing master

John Suckling, English inventor of cribbage

Izaak Walton, English author and fisherman

INDUSTRY/BUSINESS

Francis Drake, English explorer and admiral

Thomas Gresham, English founder of the Royal Exchange in London

John Hawkins, English naval commander and slave trader

Philip Henslowe, English starch manufacturer, moneylender, and theater owner

Henry Hudson, English navigator

Walter Raleigh, English explorer, author, and courtier

John Smith, English sailor and soldier, helped establish Jamestown

Thomas Sutton, English businessman, civil servant, and moneylender

SHAKESPEARE

in an
hour

AN ORDINARY LIFE

Imagine if, in some dusty corner of a forgotten room, the autobiography of William Shakespeare were found. It would, no doubt, be considered the most valuable book in the world, filled with the facts and observations for which lovers of Shakespeare — actors, scholars, historians, and playgoers — have longed. We might learn, for instance, how he made his way from a glover's shop in Stratford to the center of the theatrical world. We might know if he was a covert Catholic in a Protestant state, or if he ever traveled outside of England. Suppose it were the kind of tell-all memoir modern readers devour. We might discover who the "fair youth" and "dark lady" of the Sonnets were, how deep his grief was at the death of his young son, or what he said to his wife and children as he left them to go to the city and try his luck as an actor.

Though no such manuscript is likely to turn up, we should remember that we have more information about Shakespeare than we have of most of his contemporaries. Approximately fifty-three

---

This is the core of the book. The essay places the playwright in the context of his or her world and analyzes the influences and inspirations within that world.

documents and records survive that mention the playwright either directly or indirectly. More name members of his immediate family. They are mostly records of baptisms and marriages, sales of houses and property, appearances in court, and simple legal requests. These, along with remarks by other writers, give us a basic story. A glover's son born in Stratford makes a name for himself as a playwright in London. He becomes moderately wealthy and returns to Stratford, where he dies. This is nothing like the aristocratic life and battlefield death of the poet Sir Philip Sidney, nor the secret government missions and violent end of playwright Christopher Marlowe. Though we may long for glamour or intrigue in Shakespeare's biography — some going so far as to suggest that someone else wrote the plays — it is not particularly extraordinary. But we have his plays, and they are quite extraordinary indeed.

STRATFORD

Stratford-upon-Avon was an important market town, one hundred miles northwest of London in Warwickshire, surrounded by farmland and woods, situated on the bank of the Avon River. William's grandfather, Richard, farmed and raised livestock in nearby Snitterfield, on land rented from Robert Arden. William's father, John, left both Snitterfield and farming.

By 1552 John Shakespeare was living in Stratford, where he was fined a shilling — two days' wages for an artisan — for keeping an unauthorized dung heap in front of his Henley Street house. He was supposed to use the communal dung heap at the end of the road. Such was life in sixteenth-century Stratford. John learned the trade of a glover, which including making both simple and elaborate hand wear, as well as aprons, purses, and other soft leather goods. His business ventures expanded to include timber, real estate, and barley (ale making being the chief industry in Stratford). He also ventured into illegal wool trading (wool being a highly regulated market at the time).

In 1557 or 1558 he married Mary Arden, daughter of his father's landlord. Little is known about Mary, the playwright's mother, but certainly her father was especially fond of her. Mary was the youngest of eight siblings and four step-siblings. Yet she not only received the most generous inheritance of land after her father's death in 1556, but was also named an executor of his estate.

John and Mary Shakespeare had a fine middle-class household. John bought houses and land in Stratford, including one next to his Henley Street home, eventually joining the two to create one large dwelling. He became active in civic affairs, holding the offices of chamberlain, town council member, and alderman. In 1568 he became High Bailiff, an office roughly equivalent to mayor.

According to the baptismal records of Stratford's Holy Trinity Church, William Shakespeare was christened on April 26, 1564. Tradition has placed his birthday three days prior. Since April 23 is both the day of Shakespeare's death and the feast day of Saint George, patron of England, Shakespeare's life had both symmetry and saintly imprimatur. He would be the eldest surviving child of eight. Two girls who preceded William died in infancy.

It was a difficult year in Stratford, especially for children. The plague cut a swath through the town. The Shakespeares's Henley Street neighbors, the Greens, lost all four of their children to the disease. John and Mary would have five more children: Gilbert, who became a haberdasher; Joan, the only one other than William to marry; Anne and Richard, who lived to ages seven and thirty-eight respectively; and Edmund, born when William was fourteen. Only Edmund followed his older brother into the theater, becoming an actor.

SIXTEENTH-CENTURY ENGLAND

Daily life in sixteenth-century Stratford did not require most people to travel outside the town. Nonetheless, as changes came, they were felt in Stratford as well as in London. A year or two after John and Mary wed, Elizabeth I took the throne. She inherited a realm dizzy with the see-saw of religion, giddy with the headiness of expansion and discovery, and suspicious of its Continental neighbors. Her birth coincided with her father's creation of a Protestant England, a result of his marriage to Anne Boleyn, Elizabeth's mother. But Henry VIII's split with the Roman Catholic Church was not simply a matter of royal impetuousness.

Henry had been an opponent of religious reform, even writing a criticism of Martin Luther. His problem was that after nearly twenty-four years of marriage to Catherine of Aragon his only progeny was the princess Mary. He had no male heir. The marriage itself had required Henry to obtain a papal dispensation, for Catherine was his brother's widow and Leviticus warned that "if a man takes his brother's wife, it is an unclean thing." Growing restless and with more than an eye on the beautiful lady-in-waiting Anne Boleyn, Henry appealed to the pope to dissolve the unclean marriage. Clement VII, who had honored Henry with the title "Defender of the Faith," might have done it. However, he was more or less a prisoner of Charles V, the Holy Roman Emperor and king of Spain, who was also Catherine of Aragon's nephew. Some of Henry's advisers, eager to bring the Reformation to England, helped to craft a solution: break from Rome. And so Henry and parliament did just that.

Henry's marriage to Catherine was voided and his union with Anne validated. He was made head of the Church of England, and all church properties were confiscated from Rome and fell under his control. The English Reformation was underway, in an act that was at once personal, political, and religious.

Anne Boleyn gave Henry another daughter, Elizabeth. So Anne Boleyn was dispatched, beheaded actually, on a charge of adultery. She was replaced by Jane Seymour, who died after giving birth to the future Edward VI. Henry's church still adhered to many of the fundamental principles of the Old Faith, as it was called, but Edward was shaped by tutors decidedly more Calvinist than his father. When

Edward became king on his father's death in 1547, he instituted drastic religious changes.

After only six years on the throne, Edward died and his devoutly Catholic half-sister, Mary, became queen. She swiftly tried to reverse the changes made by Edward and was so fierce in her persecution of those who would not return to Catholicism that she earned the name "Bloody Mary." But Mary's reign came after twenty years of reform, and many of her subjects knew only the church of her father and half-brother. To them, England was Protestant. When Mary wed Prince Philip of Spain, she validated what many believed: Catholicism equaled foreign influence. When Mary died in 1558, and the twenty-five-year-old Elizabeth became queen, her first order of business was religion.

PROTESTANT QUEEN

Another woman on the throne was worrisome to some. A few thought a female monarch was against God and Nature. But those eager to return to their Protestant ways of worship rejoiced, as did those who welcomed a wholly English monarchy. Not everyone celebrated, however. Many Catholics kept their faith despite the danger. Some Protestants were dismayed at Elizabeth's lack of zeal in stripping the church of Roman elements. They hoped the extreme changes preached by reformers outside of England would take hold in Elizabeth's realm. These Protestants, who looked for a church "purified" of Catholic practices, were given the derogatory name "Puritans." Elizabeth was not interested in extremes, however. She walked a middle ground, returning the Church to the Protestantism of her father.

In Stratford, Shakespeare's father carried out his duties as alderman by issuing the expenses for the transformation of Stratford's chapel. Murals of St. George and the Dragon and of Christ and the Last Judgment were painted over. The altar was replaced with a communion table. The stained glass was removed. All were remnants of the Old Faith. Church attendance was made compulsory and recusants punished with fines, but Elizabeth was not interested in inquisitions as long as her subjects outwardly conformed. On either side of her middle way, Catholics and Puritans were theoretically allowed to hold to their beliefs, as long as they were quiet about it and went to the Established Church on Sundays.

As we have seen, however, religion was not merely a matter of spiritual concerns, but of politics and foreign affairs as well. In 1570 Pope Pius IV officially excommunicated Elizabeth, absolving her subjects of any allegiance to her. From the pulpits of churches across England, Elizabeth had her *Homily Against Disobedience* read. It warned that rebellion, even against a tyrant, is the greatest of sins against God. Catholic Spain continued to threaten. Catholic earls in the North rebelled. A plot against Elizabeth was uncovered, for which her Catholic cousin, Mary Queen of Scots, lost her head. Elizabeth's tolerance gave way to more active surveillance and persecution. Though the Puritans were surely as much of a threat to the monarchy as Catholics were, Catholicism, with its ties to foreign powers, seemed unpatriotic.

In Elizabeth's England there was much to be patriotic about. Not only had England become the center of the Reformation, it was becoming a major center of trade, industry, discovery, and creativity. Explorers brought back exotic treasures such as potatoes, tomatoes, and tobacco from the Americas. Elizabeth kept foreign powers at bay. Her refusal to marry kept the nagging question of succession in people's minds, but by declining the hands of foreign princes she kept England English. Juggling suitors from abroad, in matches proposed entirely for political possibilities, she remained a "Virgin" queen, for whom poets and courtiers crafted a kind of secular cult of adoration and respect.

STRATFORD SCHOOLING

Back in Stratford, around 1571, while Elizabeth pretended she would marry the Duke of Anjou, Shakespeare entered the King's New School in Stratford. He first would have attended the petty school, for the youngest boys. Sitting there he would have learned his ABCs from a hornbook — a wood frame enclosing a sheaf a paper with the alphabet and the Lord's Prayer covered with a thin piece of transparent horn. He would also have been taught psalms, devotions, the catechism from the Book of Common Prayer, reading, and writing, though the latter was an inexact subject at best. Elizabethan spellings ranged widely, and often had as much to do with the whims of the writer than with any rules. Shakespeare, for instance, is spelled Shakespear, Shackspeare, Shakspeyr, Shagspeare, and Shaxpaire, in different documents. The first English dictionary would not be published until 1604.

After petty school, around age ten, William would have begun grammar school, which taught just that — grammar. But it was Latin grammar. The main charge of the university-educated schoolmasters was to instill Latin grammar in the young scholars through rote learning and through reading the works of Ovid, Aesop, and Cicero. The curriculum also included rhetoric, logic, poetry, and eventually moral philosophy and Greek. Both the reading and the performing of plays were a part of the instruction, and so Shakespeare and his contemporaries were thoroughly familiar with the works of the Roman dramatists.

The evidence of this education is clear. The dramaturgy of playwrights Plautus, Terence, and Seneca was imprinted on Elizabethan writers. The figures of grammar-school history — Julius Caesar, Marc Antony, and Cleopatra — would fascinate the adult Shakespeare as well as his audience. Ovid's *Metamorphosis* was also influential. Its stories can be found throughout Shakespeare's work. Pyramus and Thisbe appear in *A Midsummer Night's Dream* and Proserpina in *The Winter's Tale*. Venus and Adonis are the subject of the poem by the same name.

COVERT CATHOLIC?

Young William Shakespeare was certainly familiar with the beliefs and rituals of the Church of England. He received religious instruction by the local clergyman and in school. The true religious affiliation of Shakespeare's family is unclear, however. Shakespeare's third cousin on his mother's side, Edward Arden of Warwickshire, was a prominent Catholic who was executed for plotting against the queen when William was eleven. In 1591, when the Queen's Privy Council wanted to take stock of the nation's spiritual and political life, it asked for lists of recusants from each parish. The playwright's father, John, was reported for his absences. At least two of Will's schoolmasters, Simon Hunt and John Cottom, were Catholic.

None of this means that Shakespeare was a Catholic. John's absence at church is explained in those same documents as being caused by his fear of arrest for debts. Having distant Catholic relations, even high-profile ones, or Catholic schoolteachers, was not unusual at the time, when at least 5 percent of the population maintained the practices of the Roman Church.

A mysterious document, found in 1757, complicates the picture, however. Over 150 years after John Shakespeare's death, during a renovation of the Henley Street home, a bricklayer found stuffed in the rafters his spiritual will and testament — a Catholic profession of faith in fourteen articles. It was a standard form letter. Counter-Reformation missionaries distributed them to large crowds of secret Catholics in not-so-secret meetings. The spiritual will suggests John was a covert Catholic. Yet little is known about William's religious beliefs. His work contains ideas and practices of the Roman faith. He refers to purgatory in *Hamlet* and confession in *Measure for Measure*. He also expressed anti-Catholic sentiments in his depiction of St. Joan in *Henry VI* and jokes about Jesuit "equivocators" in *Macbeth*. It is easy to find Christian concepts in the plays, but impossible to prove sectarian prejudice.

In Elizabeth's England, people found ways to negotiate and accept the complicated religious landscape. They knew that the winds of politics and the whims of personality could shift official doctrines quickly, as they had with Elizabeth's father and half-siblings. The safest path was the spiritual middle ground and secular conformity that Elizabeth had anticipated and allowed. Was this Shakespeare's path? The rituals of the church were one thing, religion and theology another, and faith still another. Best to make a show of the first and keep your head down about the rest.

APPRENTICE

Finishing at the King's New School around 1579 or 1580, at age fifteen or so, William would have been expected to do something. Those with money, aristocratic connections, or overwhelming desire would eventually go to university. There is no evidence, however, that William had a college career. Most likely he was apprenticed to his father, learning to make gloves, prepare leather, and be a shrewd businessman. Or rather, he was learning that the world can be a difficult place for a businessman, shrewd or not.

Three years before William's graduation, John Shakespeare stopped attending meetings of the town council, which he once presided over as High Bailiff. After twenty years of civic service, he stopped paying for the upkeep of the constables and the relief of the poor. In 1579 he mortgaged his wife's estates and avoided the sheriff on Sundays. He was in serious debt. The seventeenth-century biographer John Aubrey recorded in his *Brief Lives* the legend that William was apprenticed to a butcher, but that seems unlikely. If he was apprenticed to anyone, it makes sense that during a hard time he would have helped with the family business.

What else might Shakespeare have done following graduation? A common story is that he worked as a schoolmaster. Another is that he worked as a lawyer's clerk, given the numerous references in his works to leasing and ownership and his penchant for legal jargon.

The most tantalizing hypotheses map out a biographical road from his grammar school boyhood to the center of the London theater scene, trying to imagine when and where young Will was first bitten by the theatrical bug.

Shakespeare's earliest theatrical experience may have been as a young boy, traveling to Coventry for the Feast of Corpus Christi to see the medieval mystery plays. "Mystery" (a Middle English term derived from the Latin *ministerium*, meaning an occupation or office) refers to the trade guilds, such as carpenters, goldsmiths, and so on, who produced and performed in the pageants. Amateur players performed religious scenes of moral and spiritual instruction. Their histrionics were highly entertaining.

By the time Shakespeare was sixteen, many professional acting troupes had toured to Stratford. These included Worcester's Men, the Queen's Men, Leicester's Men, Warwick's Men, Lord Strange's Men, and Berkeley's Men. These were all popular companies, all protected by powerful patrons, and as their names imply, all composed entirely of men. A peculiar feature of the Elizabethan theater was that no women could perform. Female roles were taken by young men or boy actors, a holdover of medieval morality (and misogyny).

The plays were popular affairs in Stratford, with large and enthusiastic crowds breaking benches and windows in the Guild Hall. As an alderman or High Bailiff, John Shakespeare had to arrange for the performances and authorize the payment of the players. So if William attended with his father, they may have had V.I.P. seats and introductions to such actors as the great tragedian Edward Alleyn of Worcester's Men and Will Kempe, the young comedian of the Queen's Men. Did William dream of a theatrical career with one of the troupes? The record is silent. The only roles we know of Shakespeare taking between school and 1592 are those of bridegroom and father.

MARRIED WITH CHILDREN

On November 27, 1582, a marriage license was issued by the Bishop of Worchester to Willelmum Shaxpere and Annam Whateley. Two days later, a bond to protect the bishop in case things went wrong with the marriage mentions William Shagspere and Anne Hathwey. Allowing for haphazard variations in sixteenth-century spelling, both documents seem to refer to William Shakespeare of Stratford and Anne Hathaway of Shottery. Anne was twenty-six but William, at eighteen, was still a minor, which is why the bishop required the bond.

The Hathaways owned land in Shottery outside of Stratford. Anne's father, Richard, died a year before the wedding, and Anne brought a small dowry to the marriage. William and Anne moved into the Shakespeare house on Henley Street, which, though large, now housed William's parents, William and Anne, the glove-making shop, and five siblings. In a few months, the household would add one more.

On her wedding day, Anne was already three months pregnant, something not particularly unusual for the time. Susanna Shakespeare was born in May 1583. Her uncle, Edmund Shakespeare, one of the ten fellow inhabitants of Henley Street, had just turned three. Two years later Anne gave birth to twins, Hamnet and Judith, named after neighbors Hamnet and Judith Sadler.

It is for the period beginning in 1585, just after the birth of the twins, that one might most desire that imaginary autobiography, for the next seven years of Shakespeare's life are a blank. Perhaps he traveled, or was caught poaching deer, or perhaps he was making gloves and trading malt, scribbling bits and pieces of poems and plays when the work was slow.

The Queen's Men played Stratford in 1587, one player short, William Knell having been killed by his fellow company member John Towne in a nighttime brawl. Did William leave Stratford with the Queen's company, venturing out as an actor? All we know is that at some point he quit Stratford, leaving his wife and three children under the age of ten in the teeming house on Henley Street. He ended up in London.

LONDON

The journey to London — a two-day trip on horse, four or more days on foot — would take Shakespeare into the city though Newgate, one of the seven entrances in the stone wall surrounding the city. The wall defined the city on three sides, with the River Thames providing the south boundary. On the other side of the wall were the emerging suburbs, outside the jurisdiction of the city officials. Though Stratford was no backwater, the young Shakespeare must have thought himself in a different world — a crowded, polluted place of great variety and wonder, filled with extremes of wealth and poverty.

If he took in a deep breath of the unfamiliar London air, he would have smelled dead horses rotting in alleys, exotic perfumes from around the world, chamber pot contents thrown from windows, slaughter house offal left to run down the streets, and hundreds of species of flowers blooming in the gardens of the wealthy. In his ears would have been the sounds of horse hooves on stone, sellers hawking wares, bells from churches, songs from taverns, and conversations in English, French, Italian, and other tongues.

How quickly did he sample the huge array of foods London offered? Perhaps he bought strawberries and baked apples from a street vendor, ventured to Thames Street to buy a fruit tart, or to Leadenhall Market to marvel at the great quantities of meat. Or maybe a well-off friend invited him to a meal of turkey, a new import from America.

Touring the city, he could not miss the imposing St. Paul's Cathedral, a hub of commerce and business as well as of worship. Traveling to the east he could see the Tower, with its royal chambers, exotic menagerie, and infamous prison. To the west were the queen's palaces, Whitehall and Westminster. Some of the streets he walked would have been quite wide and clean, others were cramped alleyways through flimsy tenement homes, the signs of a city unable to accommodate a population of 200,000 and rising. It was these crowded conditions that made the plague so deadly when it came, killing 10,662 one year, and 20,136 another.

On his tour, Shakespeare might have seen a prisoner beheaded or a prostitute whipped. If he looked south at the Thames at just the right time, he might have seen the queen float by in her royal barge. On the other side of the river were brothels and bear gardens, where dogs attacked bears tied to stakes, and bulls, horses, and apes were all part of a macabre and cruel entertainment. Open spaces across the river allowed for archery competitions, games, and picnics. Beyond that lay fields and woodland.

London was a busy, energetic place, halfway between a town and a metropolis, constantly changing and growing. One thing that was growing was nationalism. It was a new and unifying force emanating from London. Shakespeare likely felt that force during the celebrations of Elizabeth's greatest military triumph — the defeat of the Spanish armada.

In 1587 Spain sent an armada of over one hundred ships to meet up with an army and attack England, but bad weather and the smaller, more maneuverable English ships combined to spell the doom of the Spanish fleet. It was an improbable victory. The small nation had sent back the more powerful foe. Seizing the moment, the triumphant Virgin Queen rode among her soldiers at Tisbury on a white horse, declaring: "I know I have the body of a weak and feeble woman, but I have the heart and stomach of a king, and a king of England too." In the face of invaders, she said, she would take up arms alongside her subjects. "I myself will be your general, judge, and rewarder of every one of your virtues in the field."

The victory added to the growing mythology of Elizabeth and to a palpable sense of patriotism in the city. London was a concentration of power, ambition, wealth, individual spirit, and entrepreneurism, the center of the Reformation and the engine of the English Renaissance. Most importantly for Shakespeare, this vibrant city was finding both expression and diversion at the theater.

THEATERS

Looking south across the Thames, Shakespeare could have also seen the newly remodeled Rose Theatre, named after the garden that once grew there. North of the city were two other theaters — the Theatre and the Curtain. These three permanent buildings catered to the growing popularity of playgoing and the resulting commercial success of the acting companies.

When acting troupes were still considered vagrants, bringing their entertainment from city to city, they would play halls, and if lucky, the manor houses of the aristocracy. They would also play market squares and inn yards. The latter provided a natural place for spectators to stand as well as balcony seats — the windows of the inn rooms themselves. In the mid-1500s some of the troupes, with increased popularity, professionalism, and noble protection, played inns in London specifically remodeled for theatrical performance. Fitted out with stages; tiring, or dressing, rooms; and stands for the audience, they had colorful names such as the Red Lion, the Bull, and Bel Savage.

To the City of London authorities, these inn theaters were a dangerous nuisance. So they tried to shut them down. One 1574 complaint against London performances contends that they lured underage girls, kept people from church, tempted the poor to waste money, attracted pickpockets and prostitutes, and drew large crowds of youth prone to fighting and illicit assignations in dark places. They also put people in constant danger of being injured by collapsing scaffolding and stage weaponry. Most importantly, crowds helped spread the plague, a constant threat in London. To the puritanical minded, acting was similar to lying and thus a sin. Boys dressed as women and ostentatious costumes offended their sensibilities as well. Armed with such arguments, officials eventually prohibited plays in inns.

The troupes, however, were not about to let London officials quell their livelihoods, especially when the demand for their art was growing at an amazing rate. In 1576 James Burbage, a carpenter turned actor, borrowed money to lease land in the north suburb of Shoreditch to build the first permanent structure solely devoted to the presentation of plays. He called it, simply, the Theatre. He chose Shoreditch because it was outside of the jurisdiction of the London city government. Rather it fell under royal authority. Those at Court, including the queen herself, enjoyed plays and did not have to worry about inn brawls, and so they offered the protection that the acting troupes and impresarios needed to build. Eventually theatrical activity would move from the north to south of the Thames, first with a theater at Newington Butts, and then with the Rose, built by the great manager, brothel-owner, and starch-maker Philip Henslowe in 1587.

INSIDE THE PLAYHOUSE

When the first outdoor theaters were constructed, the designers could look to several models. The inn yards, with some audience members standing close to the action and others situated above in the surrounding windows and balconies, served the plays well. The bear gardens accommodated large audiences focused on an event, and the theaters copied their size and shape — round or polygonal structures with several tiers of covered galleries surrounding a central pit open to the elements.

Eyewitness accounts of stage productions, along with two contemporary drawings, provide most of the information we have about the theaters. One drawing, by Henry Peachum, depicts a scene from Shakespeare's *Titus Andronicus*. It is of interest mainly because it shows a mix of costumes that is Elizabethan, Roman, and somewhere in between. The other, Dutch traveler Johannes de Witt's sketch of the

Swan Theatre, built in 1595, depicts a roughly circular open-air playhouse, with tiers of audience galleries covered by a thatched roof. In the center, in front of, and surrounding the stage is an audience area without seats, where the "groundlings" could stand. The raised stage protrudes into this area, partially covered by a ceiling supported by pillars. The back wall of the stage separates the public area from the tiring house, or backstage, in which actors changed costumes and waited for entrances. The wall has two doors on either side for entrances and exits.

Though not depicted in the DeWitt drawing, most Elizabethan playhouses probably had a large central opening in the back wall as well. This alcove, dubbed the "discovery space," served many functions. It is here that Polonius hid behind a curtain to spy on Gertrude and Hamlet and that the caskets in *The Merchant of Venice* and Desdemona's bed were revealed. Above the stage was a second level, housing musicians and serving as a balcony for *Romeo and Juliet* and other plays. It is also believed to have allowed well-paying lords a special seat to see and hear the plays.

Plays began in the afternoon, performances announced by a flag flown above the theater. Apprentices, tradesmen, and foreign visitors flocked to the playhouses, the largest of which could hold two to three thousand spectators. (They could not hold as many modern-day theatergoers, however: Elizabethans were smaller.) Food and tobacco could also be purchased at the theater, and so one imagines an atmosphere more akin to a modern baseball game than a chamber concert.

For a penny the groundlings could stand in the center section, open to the elements. For each tier of the gallery the price increased. The most expensive seats were the farthest from the stage, but the Elizabethans spoke of hearing a play rather than seeing it. As long as the actors' voices were clear, the wealthier patrons cared less about front row views than being separated from the groundlings.

The theaters were not only a popular element of urban life, they were also tourist attractions. The theater owners and acting troupes were constantly working to lure customers with new innovations and accommodations. The competition in Elizabethan London was fierce, not only from other theaters, but from the bear gardens, public executions, royal excursions, and the daily theatricality of the city itself. Interiors were painted to resemble marble, and colorful arrases decorated the buildings. Stage spectacles included trapdoors below the stage, serving as graves for Titus's sons and Ophelia. The celestially painted stage roof, called the "heavens," was equipped with a trapdoor and machinery for spectacular entrances, such as Jupiter's in *Cymbeline*. Props and scenic elements included tents, tombs, beds, hell-mouths, and possibly even painted backdrops.

Costumes could be sumptuous and expensive, many made of silk, velvet, and fur. Actors playing nobility needed to convey their wealth and rank with appropriate clothing. Some articles were obtained from nobles themselves, cast-off garments sold to the troupes by servants. Others were made specifically for the stage. As Peachum's drawing suggests, the look was generally Elizabethan, with minor historical decorations for plays set in Rome or elsewhere. Above all the costumes had to convey information about the characters, including gender, as men and boys played all the parts. They also had to engage and delight the eye. In afternoon daylight a magnificent red gown could draw attention in the way a spotlight does in the modern theater.

Eventually London would have six permanent outdoor playhouses. All this construction would not have been necessary, or possible, without the growth of the acting companies, the new business of playwriting, and the development of English drama itself.

PLAYWRIGHT

Settled in London, lodging in the ethnically diverse but dodgy neighborhood of Bishopsgate, Shakespeare worked as an actor and a playwright. How he came to act with professionals has already been addressed, but how he came to be a writer is anyone's guess.

Playwriting, being a new profession in England, was relatively open to all comers. However, aristocrats tended to find the business of theater too disreputable. A good many dramatists were, like Shakespeare, the sons of tradesmen. Ben Jonson's stepfather was a bricklayer, Christopher Marlowe's father a shoemaker, Thomas Lodge's a grocer, Anthony Munday's a draper, Henry Chettle's a dyer, and George Peele's a salter. Some enjoyed university educations, often as servitors, in which tuition was waived in exchange for remedial work. Christopher Marlowe, Thomas Kyd, Thomas Nashe, and Robert Greene all attended university. They had a network of colleagues or academic credentials to recommend them. Shakespeare did not.

Writers, however, were in demand. London had a voracious appetite for plays, and skilled men were needed to feed the theater-going beast. Managers and companies needed new works, and the smart, theater-savvy actor from Stratford was in the right place at the right time. He probably began working on scripts for hire, creating versions of already popular plays. Or he may have collaborated on scripts with a team of other writers, fixing, finishing, and doctoring existing plays, not unlike a contemporary writer's first job on a television program. For those who were skillful, quick, and clever, the writer's life offered a small financial reward, and in some cases, small bits of fame.

The going rate for a play was around £6 to £8. Ownership rested with the purchasing theater troupe, not the playwright. Plays were not protected by modern copyright laws, and companies tried to keep the plays unpublished for fear that another troupe would compete with the same play. The most popular plays were, however, printed and sold in quartos — small, quickly produced booklets called quartos because four leaves of the book were made from one large sheet of paper folded twice. Plays were not considered the kind of literature one would publish in large, impressive folio editions — at least not until Ben Jonson published his plays in 1616.

The quartos were often inaccurate or altered versions, usually sold without the consent or financial participation of the theaters or playwrights. People bought them in much the same way one can now buy bootleg DVDs of currently running movies on the streets of any major city. Many copies of Shakespeare's plays were printed, but he never saw a shilling for their publication.

THE POETIC STAGE

The early Tudor plays were mostly rough English adaptations of Plautus, Seneca, and Terrence — the old friends of English grammar school. The early playwrights were essentially amateurs writing for specialized audiences. For example, *Ralph Roister Doister*, one of the earliest Elizabethan comedies, was written by Nicholas Udall, the headmaster of Eton College. *Gorbuduc*, regarded as the first English Renaissance tragedy, was written in 1561 by two law school friends, Thomas Sackville and Thomas Norton, for their Inns of Court colleagues.

From the fifteenth-century morality plays to *Gorbuduc* is a long way. The development took seventy years or more. From *Gorbuduc* to Shakespeare's *Richard III* seems as long a way or longer. It took only thirty years — a testament to how fast English drama was changing in the sixteenth century.

Language was changing in the age of creativity and discovery. It is commonplace to say that Shakespeare gave the English language hundreds of words and phrases ("assassination," "forgone conclusion"). It is more likely that Shakespeare did not actually invent many of the words for which we give him credit, but rather was the first to write them down. He may not have even been the first, but so much attention has been paid to his works that the writer from Stratford gets the credit.

It was a time of experimentation in poetry, drama, even sermons. Shakespeare's own career is a great example of this experimentation. *Richard II, Romeo and Juliet, Hamlet, All's Well That Ends Well*, and *Cym-*

beline are very different kinds of plays. They reflect the varied thematic and formal investigations Shakespeare made. A play like *Titus Andronicus* seems so different from all his other plays that Shakespeare's authorship gets questioned. In language, structure, and content, the Elizabethan writers, Shakespeare chief among them, pushed to discover new modes of expression.

One of the most important experiments came in 1557, when Henry Howard, the Earl of Surrey, published his translation of Virgil's *Aeneid*. He did not use the usual fourteen syllables per line. Instead, he rendered it in iambic pentameter — ten syllables in each line, stress on the even ones, like a heartbeat. And it was unrhymed. Howard had "invented" blank verse. Writers thought it suited the natural rhythms of the English language better than previous forms and offered new freedom of expression. For the drama it was like trading in an old steam locomotive for a powerful new diesel. Norton and Sackville were the first to use it in the drama, but in their hands it was mechanical and monotonous. It would, however, be a magnificent engine for *The Spanish Tragedy* playwright Thomas Kyd and, especially, for Christopher Marlowe, whose Faustus famously — and iambically — asks: "Was this the face that launched a thousand ships?" Marlowe took hold of blank verse and crafted powerful, soaring works — *Tamburlaine the Great, Doctor Faustus* — of overreaching human spirit, matching spectacle with words. With Marlowe, the Elizabethan stage truly became a poetic one.

Without twenty-first-century stage technology, the Elizabethan playwrights changed locale or jumped time with an economy of words. In *Pericles* a narrator addresses the audience to explain a thirteen-year gap between scenes, but usually dialogue conveys information in Shakespeare's plays. When Troilus asked, "Why should I war without the walls of Troy / That find such cruel battle here within?", the audience knew both the place and the situation. When, at the beginning of *Hamlet*, Bernardo says, "'Tis now struck twelve. Get thee to bed, Francisco," the audience knew it was the middle of the night, despite the 2 PM sun shining into the playhouse. If the audience wanted to know what, where, and when, they first used their ears.

Place and time were not the only things made explicit in the words, however. Shakespeare's audience was not invited to engage in the kind of psychological deciphering needed for nineteenth-century realistic theater. Rather, thoughts and desires were active and on display in full glory and gruesomeness; the workings of mind and soul were expressed in the spoken word. Macbeth's lush poetry leads straight into the hell of the human heart. Iago's soliloquies expose the inner mechanics of a psychopath. And in all the plays, Shakespeare investigated love. From Helena's pretzel logic of loving and being loved in *A Midsummer Night's Dream*, to Viola's wooing "halloo" in *Twelfth Night*, to the sweet reunion of father and daughter in *Pericles*, Shakespeare gives an encyclopedic display of how lovers think and how love feels.

ACTING

As the drama developed, so too did the actors who would perform them. Out of the itinerant troupes of medieval England and players of interludes in noble houses came the acting companies of the late sixteenth century. To get around the Vagabonds Act of 1572, acting troupes had to have royal or aristocratic patronage or face arrest, especially from puritanical town officials. Bearing the name of its patron, a troupe might go on tour through the country, perform at its patron's manor, perform in London, and then play at court.

Membership in the troupes became competitive. The best had their stars. Companies jockeyed for royal favor and public reputation. Nobles sought out the finest players to carry their names. Though they were technically servants of the noble household, and required to wear its livery on special occasions, many troupes eventually organized as shareholding businesses. Then they depended more on the box office than on patronage.

As audiences saw more and more performances, they became sophisticated and discriminating consumers. Amateur oratory might serve the pasteboard speeches of *Gorboduc*. Ranting and rolling of eyes might suit the larger-than-life part of Hieronimo in the popular *Spanish Tragedy*. The poetry of Marlowe and the complex characters of Shakespeare required something else.

In *Hamlet* the title prince warns the players against the old-fashioned style of portraying Gorboducs and Hieronimos: "Speak the speech, I pray you, as I pronounced it to you, trippingly on the tongue. But if you mouth it, as many of our players do, I had as lief the town crier spoke my lines. . . . O, it offends me to the soul to hear a robustious periwig-pated fellow tear a passion to tatters, to very rags, to split the ears of the groundlings, who for the most part are capable of nothing but inexplicable dumb shows and noise." Those robustious fellows, Hamlet says, out-herod Herod. He refers to the old medieval pageants in which the part of Herod was taken on with full amateur, histrionic gusto. Acting had to become more complicated and nuanced, while still reaching the back rows of the galleries.

THE EARLY PLAYS

Whatever hack writing Shakespeare was employed in when he first arrived in London, he eventually sold his own works. Shakespeare's plays in the 1580s and early 1590s probably included *The Two Gentlemen of Verona*, *The Taming of the Shrew*, *The Comedy of Errors*, and *Titus Andronicus*. Dramatists did not often create plots out of thin air, but rather drew from a wide variety of sources, even recently popular plays. They borrowed, plundered, and combined elements at will.

For *The Two Gentlemen of Verona*, Shakespeare drew on the Spanish romance, *Diana Enamorada*, by Jorge de Montemayor. Full of puns and wordplay, *The Two Gentlemen of Verona* is a comedy of two friends, Valentine and Proteus. They venture from the title city to Milan, where the comic complications include wooing the same woman. The play includes the character of Julia, Proteus's jilted lover, who dresses as a man to become Proteus's confidante. She is the first of many Shakespearean heroines in disguise.

Though sources for *The Taming of the Shrew* are uncertain, similar themes can be found in folk literature, ballads, and other plays. We know that Shakespeare's version was popular since it was parodied by John Fletcher. Sketched with scenes of verbal fencing, wagering, and images of falconry and hunting, the marriage of Kate and Petruchio in *The Taming of the Shrew* is presented something like a sporting event. Shakespeare also dramatized an Elizabethan theory of family, namely that the husband is lord, life, keeper, and sovereign, and that subjugation to hierarchy in the familial sphere reflects the proper order of the nation and the natural order of the universe. So Kate offers her advice in the last scene of the play:

> Such duty as the subject owes the prince,
> Even such a woman oweth to her husband,
> And when she is froward, peevish, sullen, sour,
> And not obedient to his honest will,
> What is she but a foul contending rebel
> And graceless traitor to her loving lord?

A recipe for bliss, both domestic and political. Contemporary productions either embrace the Elizabethan view (such as Jonathan Miller's BBC version with John Cleese), or, more often, make Kate's capitulation another strategy in her attempt to get the upper hand.

The most "Latin" of his early plays are *The Comedy of Errors* and *Titus Andronicus*. It is no surprise that Shakespeare would turn to Plautus, Terence, and Seneca, so familiar from his school days, for inspiration. Few of his plays are as reliant on their source material as *The Comedy of Errors* is on Plautus's *Menaechmi*. Shakespeare kept the major features of the Roman farce — twins separated at a young age, a whirlwind of mistaken identities, courtesans, and charges of madness

— and re-imagined the play. He doubled the fun by doubling the twins. He upped the ante by transporting the action of the play to Ephesus, a town with a Biblical reputation for witchcraft. Modern productions often emphasize this mix of chaotic fun and dangerous magic. For example, Robert Woodruff made a circus-inspired version featuring the Flying Karamazov Brothers. The play is not only farce, however. Shakespeare shifted the comic focus from gags and bawdiness to misunderstandings between husbands and wives, which, when resolved, lead to rejuvenated love. A Palatine farce is turned into Shakespearean comedy.

Titus Andronicus was Shakespeare's answer to the bloody Roman playwright Seneca. That Roman's own plays call for a character ripping out her own womb and other such gore. Elizabethan plays such as Kyd's *The Spanish Tragedy* and Marlowe's *Tamburlaine* must have influenced him as well. He knew that violent scenes and lofty rhetorical passages were box office gold. In *Titus Andronicus*, Shakespeare crafted a wild revenge tragedy.

The story is filled with horrors. The Roman general Titus captures the Queen of the Goths. His daughter is raped and mutilated. Titus cuts off his hand. The queen unwittingly eats her sons, who have been baked into a pie. Shakespeare took part of his plot from the Procne and Philomela story in Ovid's *Metamorphosis*. Some later critics dismissed the play as being too preposterous and the language too unsubtle for Shakespeare. Another dramatist, George Peele, has sometimes been credited with writing some or most of it. Critic Harold Bloom, in *Shakespeare: Invention of the Human*, suggests it is more a parody of Marlowe's excessiveness than a serious attempt. In any case, Shakespeare found a way to compete with bearbaiting and public executions.

FAME

By 1592 Shakespeare had gained enough fame as a writer to arouse the ire of the more established dramatist Robert Greene. Greene, appealing to his fellow university-educated writers, denounced "an upstart crow, beautified with our feathers, that with his 'Tiger's heart wrapped in a player's hide' supposes he is as well able to bombast out a blank verse as the best of you." A "player's hide" makes it clear that Greene is talking about an actor-turned-playwright. The "Tiger's heart" refers to a line from Shakespeare's play *Henry VI, Part Three*. Just to be clear, Greene later refers to his target as "Shake-scene."

Greene was arguably England's first professional dramatist. The pamphlet in which his attack occurred, *Greene's Groatsworth of Wit*, was written on his deathbed. It reflects a passing of the baton, a begrudging acknowledgment that the upstart crow's star is ascendant, threatening to outshine the likes of Marlowe, Peele, and Greene himself.

From Greene's attack we also know that by 1592 Shakespeare had written at least part of a series of history plays. *Henry VI, Parts One, Two,* and *Three* and *Richard III* make up a tetrology on the English War of the Roses. Shakespeare did not invent the English history play. Yet he used the form to create masterpieces that were at once huge in scope and remarkable in detail. His main source, Raphael Holinshed's *Chronicles of England, Scotland, and Ireland*, was first published in 1577. From these Shakespeare crafted dramas that were in turns comic and tragic, with scenes of tenderness and contemplation folded among action-packed heroics.

The histories would make up fully one third of his playwriting, touching on issues of royal power and succession. Those very things were on the minds of many Londoners observing their aging, unmarried queen. In the post-armada London, tensions with France were increasing. Plays that mocked the French while playing to the jingoistic sense of Englishness would do well. The three parts of *Henry VI* and *Richard III*, with their depiction of heroism and nobility in the houses of Lancaster and York, as well as their derogatory portrayal of the French saint Joan of Arc, fit the bill.

Henry VI, Part One enjoyed success in the repertoire of Lord Strange's Men at the newly refurbished Rose Theater. It brought in more people and revenue than either Greene's *Friar Bacon and Friar Bungay* or Marlowe's *The Jew of Malta*. As a writer, Shakespeare had arrived.

PLAGUE

When the plague hit London in the summer of 1592, it closed the three playhouses. Crowded, polluted London was a welcoming home for the plague-infested rats and their disease-spreading fleas. The theaters opened in January 1593, but in February closed again. The plague eventually claimed over one thousand people a week. Actors and playwrights needed an alternate source of income. An all-star combination of the Lord Strange's Men and the Lord Admiral's Men, under the leadership of actor Edward Alleyn, toured the countryside.

Shakespeare used the time to write poetry, namely *Venus and Adonis*, *The Rape of Lucrece*, and some of the Sonnets. Shakespeare dedicated *Venus and Adonis* to the nineteen-year-old Henry Wriothesley, the Earl of Southampton. It is unclear whether Shakespeare knew Southampton before he finished the first poem. Perhaps the dedication was made with the hope of securing patronage during economically bleak times. Whatever the chronology, the poet did gain favor, as evidenced by the dedication of *The Rape of Lucrece*. "The love I dedicate to your Lordship is without end, wherof this pamphlet without beginning is but a superfluous moiety," wrote Shakespeare. "The warrant I have of your honorouble disposition, not the worth of my untutored lines, makes it assured of acceptance." The handsome allowance or other perks Shakespeare must have received from Southampton encouraged his career as a poet. He would later write *The Phoenix and the Turtle* and *The Lover's Complaint* and complete 154 sonnets.

The plague year also marked the death of Christopher Marlowe. Suspecting him of being an undercover agent for the queen, officials searched for incriminating evidence against Marlowe and in the process tortured his roommate Thomas Kyd. Though the same age as

Shakespeare, the university-educated playwright's star shone brighter sooner, perhaps spurring William on to greater accomplishments. One wonders what the course of English drama would have been if Marlowe had not been fatally stabbed with his own knife in a barroom brawl. Would he hold as important a place in history as Shakespeare does now? One thing is clear: with Marlowe's death, Shakespeare's most serious rival was gone.

THE LORD CHAMBERLAIN'S MEN

When the plague abated and Alleyn's combined touring company returned to London, their patron, Lord Strange, died. Some actors regrouped under the patronage of the Earl of Derby. Others, however, formed a new troupe under the patronage of Henry Carey, the Lord Chamberlain. The new Lord Chamberlain's Men boasted some of the best theatrical talent of the day — the tragedian Richard Burbage, the clown Will Kempe, actor and business manager Henry Condell, actor John Hemminge, and the popular actor-turned-playwright William Shakespeare. In October 1594 they began playing first in an archery range, then at the Crosskeys Inn in London. Finally they found a home at the Theatre, built and owned by Richard Burbage's father, James. They also played at court, at least twice at Christmas in that first year.

Shakespeare was a shareholder in the company, owning a stake in the company's assets. Perhaps the monetary recognition from the Earl of Southampton helped him to buy his shares. He was also the company's house dramatist and an actor — we know he at least appeared in *Sejanus* and *Every Man in His Humour*, both by Ben Jonson.

From 1594 to 1596, Shakespeare probably wrote *Love's Labour's Lost*, *Richard II*, *Romeo and Juliet*, *A Midsummer Night's Dream*, and *The Merchant of Venice* for the Lord Chamberlain's Men.

Love's Labour's Lost may have been first performed for a private audience of invited nobility, possibly at Southampton's estate. We know from the title page of the first Quarto that it was played for the queen at Christmas in 1597. The plot revolves around four young noblemen who have pledged themselves to academic pursuits to the exclusion of good food, sleep, and women. When four young women enter the picture, each quickly fall in love, abandoning the self-imposed chastity.

The couples have the wit and learning of erudite youths, the grace of Elizabethan nobility, and the poetic virtuosity of Shakespeare. The original elite audience must have appreciated the gentle satire of courtly manners and learned punning. They no doubt recognized some characters as spoofs of prominent Elizabethans. Modern audiences, however, have more difficulty unraveling this play's tangle of puns and topical references than those of any other Shakespeare play.

Like *Love's Labour's Lost*, *Richard II* is written mostly in verse. It is a story of a king who has lost the loyalty of his nobles and clings desperately to royal prerogative and divine right. It would end up being a dangerous play, used as propaganda by Essex and other would-be conspirators against Elizabeth in 1601.

Shakespeare's lyricism became more sophisticated in two plays written at the same time — *A Midsummer Night's Dream* and *Romeo and Juliet*. They are thematic twins. *A Midsummer Night's Dream* is the joyful alternative to the fatal resolution of *Romeo and Juliet*. Both plots turn on missed communications, sleeping lovers, and magic herbs in stories of young lovers drawn to each other despite parental wishes and official punishments. In *Romeo and Juliet* the Prince issues a death warrant for peace-breakers. In *A Midsummer Night's Dream* an ancient law prescribes death for disobedient daughters.

The story of Pyramus and Thisbe, from Ovid's *Metamorphoses*, hangs over both. In Ovid, the lovers' parents hate each other, and when Pyramus attempts to meet Thisbe for a secret rendezvous, he believes she is dead and therefore kills himself. In *Romeo and Juliet*, the story provides the model for the drama. In *A Midsummer Night's Dream*, Pyramus and Thisbe is the stuff of entertainment by the local workman — the mechanicals — in the play's wedding finale.

In the comedy, preposterous plans work out so that each Jack gets the proper Jill, thanks in part to the magic woods filled with fairies. Even Bottom, the weaver who is turned into an ass by the hobgoblin Puck and briefly becomes the Queen of the Fairies' lover, has a profitable end. He is given a magnificent dream to repeat and new energy with which to perform the role of Pyramus. But in *Romeo and Juliet*, all plans go awry. To deceive her family, Juliet escapes not into a magical wood, but into a tomb, relying on an absurd plan to reunite her with her husband, Romeo. The result is three dead bodies and a warning against oppressive Montagues and Capulets everywhere.

Shakespeare links the *Romeo and Juliet* story to its Italian source. He sets the play in Verona, though there is nothing particularly Veronese in the play. He sets *A Midsummer Night's Dream* in the Athens of myth, but the characters are neither Greek nor mythological, but rather his contemporaries. Even the fairies are Elizabethan.

Though a comedy, *The Merchant of Venice* becomes more problematic than comic to modern sensibilities. Bassanio's quest for the beautiful heiress Portia and the subsequent test he has to pass in order to win her is the main action of the play. Bassanio needs money for the journey. He borrows it from the Jewish moneylender Shylock, with the merchant Antonio guaranteeing the loan. When Antonio is unable to pay back the money, he owes Shylock a pound of flesh, which Shylock is ready to cut away.

Shakespeare played with the stereotypes of his time. Those who expected Shylock to be depicted in the same way as the murderous Barabbas in Marlowe's *The Jew of Malta* were in for a surprise. Shakespeare does *not* make Shylock a demon. Instead he gives him one of the most eloquent speeches on prejudice ever written. Throughout the years, the part has been played comically, sympathetically, heroically, and as part of Nazi propaganda. It is unlikely that the original audience, or Shakespeare, ever met a practicing Jew, for they had long been expelled from England. Even if it were possible for Shakespeare to have written a wholly sympathetic Shylock, it would have been bad box office.

CRISIS YEARS

In August 1596, Shakespeare's eleven-and-a-half-year-old son Hamnet died. Presumably Shakespeare returned to Stratford to bury his son at Holy Trinity Church and to comfort Anne, Susanna, and Judith. Perhaps fathers and sons were on his mind, and twins as well. Over the next four years he wrote of surrogate fathers and prodigal sons in *Henry IV*. He used a variant of his son's name, Hamlet, in the tragedy of a father-obsessed prince. Also, he crafted a comedy of a young woman who takes on the disguise of her twin bother, whom she believes dead, in *Twelfth Night*.

The following January another crisis came, this time a professional one. The lease expired on the land on which the Theatre sat, and negotiations between James Burbage and the landlord did not go well. Searching for a new home, Burbage bought the rectory of the Blackfriars monastery and had it fitted out as a theater. The monastery was within London's city walls, but, as former church land, fell within the jurisdiction of the Crown and not the city officials. The aristocratic neighbors, however, were not pleased with the prospect of having a theater nearby — the noise, the crowds, all classes of people milling about — and persuaded the Queen's Privy Council to block its use. James Burbage died, the Theatre's landlord remained stubborn, and the Lord Chamberlain's Men were without a theater. The landlord's plans were to tear down the Theatre and put the wood, timber, and land to better use.

Financially, however, William Shakespeare was doing well. He was a successful businessman, engaged in the activities one would expect. He bought hundreds of acres of land outside of Stratford and a small cottage in the village. He sold commodities, sued people for payment, was sued himself, loaned money, made investments, and was cited for not paying his taxes.

From his theatrical activities, he may have been bringing in around £200 a year, fifteen to twenty times what a skilled artisan might earn. His Stratford dealings added at least half again as much. In 1597 he bought the second-largest house in Stratford, a brick and timber dwelling with ten fireplaces and a substantial garden, to be called New Place. Along with this substantial new dwelling came new rank. Shakespeare had applied for a coat of arms in his father's name the previous fall, and it had been granted. John Shakespeare and his son were now gentlemen. Their crest included a falcon and spear and the motto *Non san droict*, "not without right."

Between 1596 and 1598, the gentleman playwright wrote *King John, Henry IV, Parts One* and *Two*, *The Merry Wives of Windsor*, and *Much Ado About Nothing*. The success of his first history plays assured that Shakespeare would write more. For *King John*, he used Holinshed's account of England's medieval king to explore the difference between a ruler's legitimacy and ability.

In *Henry IV Parts One* and *Two*, Shakespeare picked up the story where *Richard II* left off, chronicling Henry's battles to keep his crown after his defeat of Richard. They also tell of his son, Prince Hal, whom we see in the roles of prodigal son, thief, drunk, battlefield hero, and finally, king. The plays also contain one of Shakespeare's greatest comic creations, the drunken knight and King of Liars, Sir John Falstaff. To Hal he is a surrogate father, teaching him lessons King Henry could never offer. Some of the lessons are about eating, drinking, and lying, but all are about Hal's future subjects. At Hal's coronation, Falstaff eagerly waits in the street for his former student. The new king of England, however, cannot allow the father of the comic world to penetrate into the political world. "I know thee not, old man: fall to thy prayers," he says to Falstaff, as he banishes his tavern tutor.

It is said that Elizabeth so loved Falstaff that she requested a third play with him, showing the knight in love. It seems like a ridiculous request to come from the queen, but clearly someone had the idea. Some of the lines suggest that the third Falstaff play, *The Merry Wives of Windsor*, was written for the 1597 Order of the Garter Ceremony at Windsor, which Elizabeth attended. Plucked out of the fourteenth-century reign of Henry IV, Falstaff is transported to the Elizabethan countryside in a romantic comedy spiced with slapstick and silliness.

Romantic comedy and the wit of *Love's Labour's Lost* find a more mature plot and more fully developed sparring partners in *Much Ado About Nothing*. Unlike the earlier play, it is written mostly in prose. Shakespeare borrowed from Ariosto's *Orlando Furioso* and Edmund Spenser's *Faerie Queene* for his plot. His heroine is, however, from Greek legend — a beautiful youth who jumps, grief-stricken, to a watery death — rendered by Marlowe in the poem *Hero and Leander*. Shakespeare's Hero fakes her death to punish her fiancé, Claudio, who has been tricked by his sinister half-brother Don John into publically denouncing Hero's faithfulness. Against this story, Shakespeare sets the courtship of Hero's cousin Beatrice and the officer Benedict. They are two hardheaded, sharp-witted, cynical souls, who argue against romantic love and dewy-eyed silliness. Their sparring is the most memorable part of the play. It anticipates such quick-witted couples as Elizabeth Bennet and Mr. Darcy and numerous Hepburn and Tracy films.

The farcical constable Dogberry and his men stumble upon Don John's plot, allowing for a happy ending. Claudio is repentant. Hero is forgiving. Beatrice and Benedict become engaged, and Don John is apprehended. The comedy's language is rich in puns, malapropisms, and double entendres. All mirror the larger theme of appearance versus reality, deception versus truth.

THE GLOBE

On the night of December 28, 1598, James Burbage's sons, Cuthbert and Richard, gathered a group of friends, carpenters, and workmen to dismantle the Theatre. They brought the timber across the Thames by ferry and reassembled it at Bankside. They had thwarted the Shoreditch landowner and constructed the most famous theater in history, the Globe.

Already a shareholder in the acting company, Shakespeare became a shareholder in the Globe as well, originally with a 10 percent interest. The shareholders put up the money to rent the land and build the new theater, and they would share in the profits.

By autumn 1599 the Globe was opened, flying a flag of Hercules holding up the world. One of the first plays was surely *Henry V*, in which the Chorus welcomes the patrons to the splendid new playhouse, wondering if the "vasty fields of France" can be crammed with the "wooden O."

By 1600, in a city of just over 200,000, the Globe was one of at least five large outdoor theaters, along with the Curtain, the Rose, the Swan, and the Fortune. Fifteen thousand patrons visited the playhouses each week. Performing the plays were professional companies, who appeared daily save Sundays, Lent, and when the plague forced them closed.

Shakespeare's reputation grew even more. Francis Meres, in *Palladis Tamia*, published in 1598, praised the "mellifluous and honeytongued" Shakespeare's "rare ornaments and resplendent habiliments." His plays drew in the crowds, and the Lord Chamberlain's Men and the Globe prospered, whether they were playing one of their house writer's works, or plays by other dramatists.

Plays at the Globe from 1599 to 1604 included *Julius Caesar, As You Like It, Hamlet, Twelfth Night, Troilus and Cressida, Measure for Measure*, and *All's Well That Ends Well*. Shakespeare also had a hand in the play *Sir Thomas More*. His contributions to it were slight — at least five writers worked on the play. It was probably never performed in Shakespeare's day, due to the delicate nature of portraying a Catholic martyr in the realm of the aging Elizabeth.

For *Julius Caesar*, Shakespeare used Sir Thomas North's translation of Plutarch's *Lives of the Noble Grecians and Romans Compared Together*. In Shakespeare's hands, the political melodrama was made interesting because no character is wholly one thing or another. The great ruler Caesar is a braggart who suffers from epilepsy and deafness. Brutus is motivated by pure intentions as well as a vague notion that he holds the reins of history. Marc Anthony seems a familiar political figure, whose powerful, empathetic speech gains support from the common people. The play proceeds mostly in rather formal-sounding verse, its serious speech worthy of senators, Roman or otherwise.

The world of politics and power is portrayed as unnatural and cruel in the comedy *As You Like It*. The play contrasts a callous and pretentious court, from which both familial and romantic love are banished, against the Forest. There the rightful Duke lives like Robin Hood with his men, a testament to simplicity and loyalty. Forests are usually magical places in Shakespeare's work, and the forest in *As You Like It* has an extra pedigree. It bears Shakespeare's mother's maiden name.

One of Shakespeare's greatest heroines, the smart and energetic Rosalind, lives disguised as a man in the Forest of Arden after she is banished by her uncle, the usurper of her father's dukedom. Rosalind's suitor, Orlando, also ends up there, hanging love-sick poems on the trees. The disguised Rosalind uses the opportunity to test and tutor Orlando's love. By the end of the play there are four couples, a set of reunited brothers, and the Duke called out of exile. The play contains the famous speech, spoken by the melancholic Jaques, one of the Duke's exiled men: "All the world's a stage/and all the men and women merely players." It expresses the idea of *theatre mundi* — the stage as the world and the world as a stage — that intrigued renaissance audiences and artists. Why else call your theater the Globe?

DEATH OF A FATHER

In 1601, Shakespeare's father, John, died. In addition to his other Stratford properties, Shakespeare now owned the Henley Street house, where his mother still lived. He had become the head of the family. Traveling back to Stratford to bury his father, was Shakespeare thinking about the play he was writing, whose title echoed the name of his own dead son?

Hamlet is the greatest of all revenge tragedies, a popular form in Shakespeare's day. It is large and sprawling, and the texts that survive are probably too long to have been played in their entirety. Maybe the published texts are really conglomerations of several different performance versions. Or maybe the spirit of experimentation led Shakespeare to write an unstageable play. Whatever the history, it is a singular achievement, tracing the contortions of thought of Hamlet as he grieves, strategizes, and reinterprets his own life.

Beginning with the appearance of Hamlet's dead father at the beginning of the play, Hamlet has his mission — to kill his father's murderer, sending the killer's soul to hell. His mother has married his killer-uncle, and, whatever else they are, they are also the king and queen. Hamlet's revenge is personal, political, and spiritual. He must negotiate between his private agony and his public face. He needs both proof and time, and so concocts a scheme worthy of an overeducated, grief-stricken prince in a comedy: he acts crazy.

Hamlet may sprawl, but it is a good example of Shakespeare's control of the dramatic elements. One strategy he uses is to put two different "clocks" in the drama. One clock marks the reasonable or logical amount of time it takes the story to unfold. The other clock is a dramatic one, following a story that begins logically until "time is out of joint." With the dramatic clock the action speeds up, slows to a crawl, and speeds up again before returning to logical time again in the fifth act, in which the duel seems to be mercilessly in real time, bringing death upon death and finally a new political order.

Shakespeare moved from the gloomy Elsinore to the fictional Mediterranean Illyria for *Twelfth Night, or What You Will*. At its center are the twins Viola and Sebastian. They are separated by a shipwreck, each thinking the other is dead. Viola disguises herself in her brother's clothes, finding work in the court of Duke Orsino, who is in a mock-melancholic mood over his unrequited love for the Countess Olivia.

Viola soon becomes the messenger between the two. "Are you a comedian?" asks Olivia, wondering if Viola is an actor. In *Hamlet* acting has the purpose to revenge a murder, in *Twelfth Night* it leads to love.

Viola is quick, observant, and expressive, and both Orsino and Olivia fall for this girlish boy, but Viola has eyes only for the Duke. Remember that Viola was a boy actor playing a girl dressed as a boy, delighting the audience with the layered sexual tensions of the love-chase.

A rival for Olivia's love is the silly Sir Andrew Aguecheek. He is spurred on by Olivia's relative Sir Toby Belch, a rowdy knight who loves late-night parties. When Olivia's puritanical steward, Malvolio, tries to break up the fun, Toby and his cohorts trick him into believing Olivia is in love with him. Sebastian turns up in Ilyria. Because he and his sister look so much alike, confusion ensues. Viola finally realizes that her twin is not, in fact, dead. She reveals her love for the Duke, and her brother falls in love with Olivia. At the end, with weddings imminent, Malvolio storms away vowing revenge.

Named after the Christmas season's Feast of the Epiphany, on which rules were turned upside down and servants lorded over masters, *Twelfth Night* is a completely secular romp. The penetrating investigation of character and poetic artistry of *Hamlet* are also found in the comedy. Though Shakespeare littered the final scene with married couples rather than bodies, some of the melancholy of the tragedy seeped into *Twelfth Night*. Its final song reminds everyone that the "rain it raineth every day."

Between 1602 and 1603 Shakespeare wrote *Troilus and Cressida*, *Measure for Measure*, and *All's Well That Ends Well*. A few modern critics labelled them "problem plays" because they contain a central "problem" or moral dilemma for one or more characters. The three plays are not easily classified as comedy or tragedy. They defy pigeonholing.

The central question of *Troilus and Cressida*, set during the Trojan War, is how the value of any person, idea, or thing can be determined. Troilus prizes the beautiful Cressida, but she soon betrays him. Hector thinks Helen is not worth the war, but the other Trojans want to battle on. Achilles, his pride wounded, tries to sit out the war, but exacts bloody revenge when the fighting affects him personally. Filled with less-than-heroic heroes and less-than-romantic lovers, the play also contains eloquent argument and debate.

Isabella, a nun, might save her brother's life if she sleeps with his oppressor in *Measure for Measure*. The harsh Angelo is allowed to rule as the real Duke passes disguised through the city. Claudio is sentenced to death by Angelo for sexual indiscretions, forcing Isabella into her dilemma. The disguised Duke helps Isabella play a trick on Angelo by substituting Angelo's spurned lover Mariana in the bed. It is a dark comedy, turning on moments of moral decisions and mercy.

All's Well That Ends Well revolves on a similar bedtrick. The heroine, Helena, substitutes herself for another woman in an attempt to make her fiancé, Bertram, recognize his bond to her, despite his disgust at her low social status. Taken from the *Decameron* via William Painter's English adaptation, called *The Palace of Pleasure*, it is a cynical fairy tale. Helena wins her claim on Bertram by miraculously saving a dying king. One wonders if Shakespeare thought at all about a parallel to his own dying monarch.

LONG LIVE THE KING

The first months of 1603 began with the decline of England's sixty-nine-year-old ruler. Afraid to lie down, she remained constantly seated. In February, the Lord Chamberlain's Men played before her at court. By March she was dead. The ring symbolizing her marriage to the country she had ruled for forty-three years was embedded in her finger and had to be cut away.

The nagging national question of who would succeed the childless queen was answered by Elizabeth herself. She wanted to be followed by a king and a kinsman, her cousin James, King of Scotland. Fearing that his mother, Mary Queen of Scots, was the center of conspiracies,

Elizabeth had reluctantly had her executed sixteen years before. Now the son was to become James I of England. No blood was shed; there was only cheering in the streets. When James rode into London to be crowned, the plague raged, the theaters were closed, and the public coronation ceremonies were postponed until spring of the following year.

James had assumed the Scottish throne as a boy while his mother was imprisoned in England. The young man, bow-legged and of medium build, was particularly fond of hunting and golf. It was, however, his intelligence and proficiency in Greek, Latin, theology, and cosmology that delighted the Scottish court and would shape the interests and politics of the adult King James.

An effective ruler of Scotland for twenty-five years, his ascent to the English throne was welcomed by many who had grown weary of Elizabeth's rule. The queen, however, left a legacy of precarious royal finances, growing inflation, restless nobility, and religious tensions waiting to erupt. James was a peace-loving, pedantic, and financially imprudent ruler. The country's problems proved too difficult for him. He became increasingly unpopular. The memory of Elizabeth's reign took on the golden patina of nostalgia.

Called the wisest fool in Christendom by his detractors, he was the most literary king ever to rule England. James fashioned himself as a thoughtful, philosophical ruler, who nourished literature and the sciences. He was a writer, poet, critic, a staunch hater of tobacco and witches, and a defender of the Divine Right of kings. He would oversee the publication of the Authorized Version of the Bible, which would forever carry his name.

James was also a patron of the theater, dance, and other entertainments. The playwright Ben Jonson collaborated with the architect and designer Inigo Jones to create elaborate court masques. These amalgamations of poetry, music, allegorical characters, and lavish costumes were written especially for royal festivities. The king wanted the very best theatrical troupe as his own. He quickly became the patron of

Shakespeare's company, which would be known as the King's Men. They would play at the court of James roughly four times more often than at the court of Elizabeth.

We think of Shakespeare as an Elizabethan. Yet some of his greatest works were, in fact, Jacobean. They included a great string of tragedies: *Othello*, *Timon of Athens*, *King Lear*, *Macbeth*, *Antony and Cleopatra*, and *Coriolanus*.

TRAGIC OUTSIDERS

Written during James's first year as king, *Othello, the Moor of Venice* is a domestic drama. Shakespeare drew from a story by Giraldi Cinthio about a Moorish general who is led to murder his young wife, Desdemona, through the machinations of his ensign. Shakespeare turned what could have been a melodramatic romance into a fast-paced descent of a great man into a jealous fury. He allowed no moment for passions to cool, misunderstandings to be cleared up, or lies to be challenged. The play is fueled by the outsider status of Othello, but driven by the strategies of a malcontent, Iago.

Iago is the third-longest role in Shakespeare. Like Hamlet, he spends a lot of time in soliloquy, revealing his intellectual gymnastics, the very process of his thinking, and the degrees of his loathing. Why does Iago hate? Shakespeare gives a bounty of reasons. None is wholly sufficient. Perhaps the dramatist is attempting what Dostoyevsky would do centuries later — to crack open the skull of a murderer and inspect the gears.

The first recorded performance of *Othello* was for King James in 1604. Richard Burbage, in black face, played the title role. For Shakespeare's audience the idea of race was only emerging as a concept. *Moor* could mean Moroccan, Arab, or anyone from anywhere on the African continent. The stereotype was of a jealous and unpredictable exotic who was also an insatiable sexual predator. Though there were Moorish businessmen in London, and the Moroccan ambassador paid a six-month visit to Elizabeth's court, the typical stage Moor was a black-faced villain bent on destruction, an object of fear and fascination. As he did with Shylock, Shakespeare both used and confounded expectations. He created a noble, loving, and just Othello, who is nonetheless drawn into jealous tyranny and savagery, fulfilling the stereotype.

White actors continued to play Othello in dark makeup into the twentieth century. The blacked-up Othellos of Laurence Olivier and Orson Welles were recorded on film. In the mid-nineteenth century James Hewlett in the United States and Ira Aldridge in England were among the first black actors to play the part. Today the role is most often taken by actors of color.

In *Timon of Athens*, nominally set in ancient Greece, Shakespeare fashioned one of his oddest tragic heroes. Generous, foolish, and self-centered, Timon gives his wealth away to all comers. When his fortunes are spent and creditors are at the door, he turns to his so-called friends, all of whom refuse to help him. Disgusted with mankind, he leaves society to live in the wilderness, where he rails against the hypocrisy of fellow human beings. And it is there he dies, angry and alone, still misperceiving — he was never as loved nor as despised as he thought. Perhaps written with Thomas Middleton, it is a sharp critique of greed and materialistic doom. One wonders why it is not produced more often in contemporary times.

An even bleaker vision of the world is presented in *King Lear*, set in medieval Britain. Lear decides, in his old age, to divide his kingdom among his three daughters. Before he transfers power, he subjects each to a test, saying he will offer the largest portion to the one who loves him best. While Goneril and Regan fawn on their father, Cordelia enrages him with her truthfulness and is disinherited. Lear soon sees his foolishness. Goneril and Regan grow despotic, their love for Lear proves false, and their ambition is unchecked. The kingdom becomes unhinged, and so does Lear. His profound descent into "madness," the startling world of cruelty and betrayal, and the final, terrible image of

Lear carrying the dead Cordelia in his arms are unparalleled anywhere else in Shakespeare's tragic vision.

The play is especially interesting because it highlights the problems with landing on one accepted text for study or performance. Three published versions vary greatly. The first Quarto contains 285 lines not found in the Folio. The Folio has 100 lines not found in the first Quarto. While modern editors traditionally publish a conglomeration of the Quartos and Folio, some, such as the Oxford Shakespeare, publish a Quarto and a Folio version as separate texts.

HISTORICAL TRAGEDIES

A play set in Scotland featuring witches seems a good choice to play before James I. As king of Scotland, he wrote the treatise *Daemonologie* and oversaw the trials of witches thought to have tried to assassinate him. The play's depiction of evil forces overthrowing a king would also remind Shakespeare's audience of the remarkable Gunpowder Plot of 1605. That was a plan by Guy Fawkes and his fellow Catholic conspirators to blow up the king and parliament.

Not as gory as *Titus Andronicus*, but "steeped in blood" nonetheless, *Macbeth* is a horror show, with a trio of witches to set the terror in motion. Once Macbeth murders Duncan to gain the crown, he never stops killing. While he is despicable, he also has soliloquies that elicit sympathy for his poetic, tortured soul.

The stage Macbeth is very different than the one of history, who was an able monarch, military leader, and patron of the church. In Holinshed's *Chronicles*, Banquo is an accomplice in the murder of Duncan, but Banquo was supposedly an ancestor of James. Shakespeare paints him as an innocent and honorable nobleman. The historical Macbeth's wife, Gruoch, is a poor model for Lady Macbeth; Shakespeare was more influenced by Seneca's *Medea*.

One character that comes from theatrical tradition and not history is the Porter, a combination of the Porter of Hell-Gate character from the medieval mystery plays and a sort of Jacobean Richard Pryor, weaving political and social commentary into a short comic sketch. In the eighteenth century, producers cut the Porter's scene, distressed at its unrefined tone. But Shakespeare knew what he was doing. After the short comic interlude, when the Porter finally lets Macduff and Lennox into Macbeth's castle of murder and treason, the audience is not allowed to laugh for the rest of the play. Besides, it gives the actor playing Macbeth time to wash off all the blood.

Theatrical lore says that the play is cursed, that mishaps and accidents plague productions and even saying the title can bring bad luck. If it is unlucky, it is probably because of its quick pace (lots of actors running about backstage), stage effects, and weaponry, making it more likely to cause injury than, say, a Sunday sermon. Just what those Puritan city officials warned about.

For his last two great tragedies, Shakespeare looked again to Roman history, in stories drawn from Plutarch's *Lives*. In *Antony and Cleopatra*, Shakespeare created a sweeping, excessive play of love and war, opposing the stoic, well-ordered Rome with Cleopatra's expressive, emotional Egypt. Shakespeare crafts many scenes, moving between the two worlds. Antony tries to exist in both, but he cannot. Though rulers of nations, the lovers end their lives not unlike their young theatrical predecessors Romeo and Juliet — Antony with a sword and the captured Cleopatra with the poison of a snake.

In *Coriolanus*, the title character, newly victorious from battle, is urged by his mother Volumnia to run for consul. He wins, but he openly despises the common people and popular rule. Banished from Rome, he returns with an army. Persuaded by Volumnia to call off an attack, he is killed as a traitor in his newly adopted city. Through controlled, formal language and careful plotting, the play feels even more classical than *Julius Caesar*. As he was writing it, Shakespeare was also experimenting with a very different kind of play, the fluid, unrestrained fairy tales that begin with *Pericles*. These, along with one last history play and a couple of collaborative tragicomedies, would

make up his last phase of writing. *Coriolanus* would be his final
tragedy.

LATE PLAYS

Shakespeare's attention was turning increasingly to matters of business,
family, and real estate back in Stratford. In 1607 his daughter Susanna
married Dr. John Hall and his brother Edmund died. The following
year his mother died and his granddaughter Elizabeth was born. It
does not seem that his theatrical activity slowed down much, however.
He continued to write and was involved in the company's purchase of
another theater. His reputation as a writer continued to shine as well
with the publication of the Sonnets.

Shakespeare had probably finished writing the Sonnets around
1603, but they were all finally printed together in 1609, without his
involvement. The publisher, Thomas Thorpe, dedicated the edition to
Mr. W. H., which has led to endless speculation about the poems'
inspiration. The first group of the Sonnets is addressed to a "fair
youth." Some find fatherly advice in the poems, others a homosexual
affair. The second group is addressed to a "dark lady" with whom the
narrator has a passionate affair. Eventually, the fair youth and the dark
lady have a relationship. The Earl of Southampton is most often put
forward as the inspiration for the fair youth (and as Henry Wriothesley, his initials are W. H. reversed). Numerous women have been
suggested for the dark lady. It is just as likely that these are invented
characters without real-life counterparts, created to serve the poet's
artistic scheme.

In 1608, the King's Men took possession of the Blackfriars
Theatre, which James Burbage had renovated and abandoned. It had
been leased to the Children of the Chapel Royal at Windsor — a boys
acting company. In the large public theaters, boys took the roles of
women and children alongside the adult actors. In the small private
children's theaters, casts were comprised entirely of student "choris-

ters" of St. Paul's, Westminster, Eton College, and the Chapel Royal. They were trained in their craft by academics. When the Chapel Royal children ran into political trouble with a play that offended the French ambassador, they vacated Blackfriars, and the King's Men acquired a second theater.

The building was small compared to the Globe, entirely indoors, and lit by candles. There were possibly two galleries, and most of the audience was seated. The more intimate setting led to differences in playing styles in the two venues; one imagines the private theater performances to be more subtle, with simple lighting effects possible with the use of candles. The company did not, however, segregate their repertoire. The same plays were produced at both theaters.

Blackfriars became the winter home of the King's Men, with the Globe for spring and summer. At 700, the Blackfriars' audience capacity was only a fourth of the Globe, but admission was six times higher. The indoor theaters were the places to see and be seen, even offering the opportunity for a finely dressed nobleman to show off his couture by sitting on the stage itself — for a fee, of course. It turned out to be a good investment, for in a short time shareholders' profits at Blackfriars were higher than those at the Globe.

The plays written between 1607 and 1611 were *Pericles*, *Cymbeline*, *The Winter's Tale*, and *The Tempest*. All feel more fluid and fantastical than the rest of his work. They are mixed bags of comedy and tragedy, featuring journeys, exiles and reunions, large gaps in time, magic, and ancient gods. The goddess Diana appears in *Pericles* and Jupiter in *Cymbeline*. The plays were labeled romances in the nineteenth century because of their similarities to medieval romance literature. They are among Shakespeare's most lyrical and theatrical works.

Shakespeare's last solo play, *The Tempest*, sets the exiled magician Prospero and his daughter Miranda on a magical island that Prospero rules. When his former enemies come near the island, Prospero creates a storm to bring them to his shores. Eventually all reconcile with Prospero, and he with them. Prepared to return to civilization to see his daughter married, Prospero breaks his magic staff and frees his servants, the spirit Ariel, and the creature Caliban.

It is hard not to think of Prospero's powers as those of a great playwright-sorcerer, conjuring storms, taming spirits, and reconciling enemies in a few hours time. The play is a beautiful farewell to a world of creation and fantasy, written in 1611, when Shakespeare himself, somewhat wealthy and rather famous, was attending less to the theater and more to investments, real estate, and the day-to-day affairs of the world.

STRATFORD AGAIN

Shakespeare bought a house in Blackfriars very near the theater in 1613. Whether he ever lived in it, or intended to live in it, is not known. It might have been an investment, for Shakespeare was now spending much of his time at New Place. He did have to go to London, but the commute from Stratford to the city was a long one. He was collaborating with John Fletcher, writing *Cardenio* (now lost); *All Is True*, or *Henry VIII*; and *The Two Noble Kinsmen*. The same year he made his Blackfriars purchase, stage cannons set fire to the thatched roof of the Globe during a performance of *Henry VIII* and the theater burned.

The Globe was rebuilt with a tiled roof, the King's Men continued to play, but Fletcher was becoming the troupe's playwright. Shakespeare's daughter Judith married Richard Quiney in February 1616, but Quiney turned out to have a host of troubles, including fathering a child with another woman (both mother and child died in childbirth). Shakespeare, not trusting his new son-in-law, revised his will so that Judith inherited a lump sum in her own name.

Two months after Judith's marriage, on April 23, 1616, Shakespeare died. His will left his family provided for — especially Susanna and her husband — and made certain his wife, Anne, would receive his second-best bed. Whether the second-best bed was actually a more loving bequest than the first-best bed has been the subject of much debate. In any case, we know she got a bed. He was buried in the chancel of Holy Trinity Church. The stone on his grave bears a warning to a sextant who might move the remains to the charnel house to make way for other bodies: "Good friend, for Jesus' sake forbear/To dig the dust enclosed here./Blessed be the man that spares these stones/And cursed be he that moves my bones."

Above the tomb a monument was placed, a stone effigy of the writer by sculptor Gerard Johnson. Though it might be a true likeness, the sculpture looks more like an alderman than a Great Poet. Or, as Shakespeare critic J. Dover Wilson said, like a "self satisfied porkbutcher." But that is to suppose aldermen or pork butchers — or glover's sons — do not make Great Poets.

THE FIRST FOLIO

In 1623, Anne Shakespeare died, and later that year The First Folio of Shakespeare's works appeared. Compiled by his friends and company members John Heminges and Henry Condell, it was a labor of love as much as it was a gift to lovers of Shakespeare's plays. It is an uneven compilation. Some plays take their texts from published quartos, others from the company's own texts. *Pericles* is left out. The page numbering is incorrect. It is, nonetheless, one of the great books of the English language. On the frontispiece is Martin Droeshout's famous engraving of Shakespeare, which looks so unlike a real person that it is hard to believe the portrait is accurate. Ben Jonson's introduction to the Folio is very accurate, though:

> Thou art a monument, without a tomb,
> And art alive still, while thy book doth live . . .
> He was not of an age, but for all time.

Though Shakespeare was gone, his plays continued to be performed, alongside those of Jonson, Fletcher, and others, even though the new elite tastes of the private theaters found his works to be of the old-fashioned kind.

It was not theatrical fashion that would drive Shakespeare from the stage, but rather politics. The Puritans gained control of parliament and sought to pare away excess and bring about responsible, moral governance to national affairs, the church, and every aspect of life. When James died in 1628, his son Charles I assumed the throne, and conflicts between the Puritans and Royalists led to civil war. The Puritans took control, and, in 1642, closed the theaters. The English Renaissance was effectively over, and the most extraordinary period of the English stage — the age of Shakespeare — had come to an end.

DRAMATIC MOMENTS

from the Major Plays

The following excerpts are from six plays — one history, three comedies, and two tragedies. Three are mostly in verse, two in prose, and one in both. They are presented here in the order of composition. Punctuation follows *The Oxford Shakespeare*, Stanley Wells and Gary Taylor, General Editors, 1987.

These short excerpts are from the playwright's major plays. They give a taste of the work of the playwright. Each has a short introduction in brackets that helps the reader understand the context of the excerpt. The excerpts, which are in chronological order, illustrate the main themes mentioned in the In an Hour essay. Premiere date is provided.

from **Henry IV, Part One** (1591–1592)

from Act Two Scene Five

CHARACTERS

> Prince Harry
> Falstaff
> Hostess

[In the tavern, Prince Harry — known familiarly as Prince Hal — and Falstaff take turns role-playing a dialogue between Harry and his father, the king. At first a comic scene, Falstaff says he will play the king as if playing in King Cambyses, a bombastic tragedy of the time. It turns serious, however, when Harry plays his father, foreshadowing Falstaff's fall from favor at the end of Henry IV, Part Two, when Harry becomes Henry V.]

PRINCE HARRY: Do thou stand for my father, and examine me upon the particulars of my life.

FALSTAFF: Shall I? Content. This chair shall be my state, this dagger my sceptre, and this cushion my crown.

(He sits.)

PRINCE HARRY: Thy state is taken for a joint-stool, thy golden sceptre for a leaden dagger, and thy precious rich crown for a pitiful bald crown!

FALSTAFF: Well, an the fire of grace be not quite out of thee, now shalt thou be moved. Give me a cup of sack to make my eyes look red, that it may be thought I have wept; for I must speak in passion, and I will do it in King Cambyses' vein.

PRINCE HARRY: (*Bowing.*) Well, here is my leg.

FALSTAFF: And here is my speech. Stand aside, nobility.

HOSTESS: O Jesu, this is excellent sport, i' faith!

FALSTAFF: Weep not, sweet Queen; for trickling tears are vain.

HOSTESS: O the father, how he holds his countenance!

FALSTAFF: For God's sake, lords, convey my tristful Queen,
For tears do stop the floodgates of her eyes.

HOSTESS: O Jesu, he doth it as like one of these harlotry players as ever I see!

FALSTAFF: Peace, good pint-pot; peace, good tickle-brain.— Harry, I do not only marvel where thou spendest thy time, but also how thou art accompanied. For though the camomile, the more it is trodden on, the faster it grows, yet youth, the more it is wasted, the sooner it wears. That thou art my son I have partly thy mother's word, partly my own opinion, but chiefly a villainous trick of thine eye, and a foolish hanging of thy nether lip, that doth warrant me. If then thou be son to me, here lies the point. Why, being son to me, art thou so pointed at? Shall the blessed sun of heaven prove a micher, and eat blackberries? — A question not to be asked. Shall the son of England prove a thief, and take purses? — A question to be asked. There is a thing, Harry, which thou hast often heard of, and it is known to many in our land by the name of pitch. This pitch, as ancient writers do report, doth defile. So doth the company thou keepest. For Harry, now I do not speak to thee in drink, but in tears; not in pleasure, but in passion; not in words only, but in woes also: And yet there is a virtuous man whom I have often noted in thy company, but I know not his name.

PRINCE HARRY: What manner of man, an it like your majesty?

FALSTAFF: A goodly, portly man, i'faith, and a corpulent; of a cheerful look, a pleasing eye, and a most noble carriage; and, as I think, his age some fifty, or, by'r Lady, inclining to threescore. And now I remember me, his name is Falstaff. If that man should be lewdly given, he deceiveth me; for, Harry, I see virtue in his looks. If, then, the tree may be known by the fruit, as the fruit by the tree, then peremptorily I speak it — there is virtue in that Falstaff. Him keep with; the rest banish. And tell me now, thou naughty varlet, tell me, where hast thou been this month?

PRINCE HARRY: Dost thou speak like a king? Do thou stand for me, and I'll play my father.

FALSTAFF: (*Standing.*) Depose me. If thou dost it half so gravely, so majestically both in word and matter, hang me up by the heels for a rabbit sucker, or a poulter's hare.

PRINCE HARRY: (*Sitting.*) Well, here I am set.

FALSTAFF: And here I stand. Judge, my masters.

PRINCE HARRY: Now, Harry, whence come you?

FALSTAFF: My noble lord, from Eastcheap.

PRINCE HARRY: The complaints I hear of thee are grievous.

FALSTAFF: 'Sblood, my lord, they are false. Nay, I'll tickle ye for a young prince, i'faith.

PRINCE HARRY: Swearest thou, ungracious boy? Henceforth ne'er look on me. Thou art violently carried away from grace. There is a devil haunts thee in the likeness of an old fat man; a tun of man is thy companion. Why dost thou converse with that trunk of humours, that bolting-hutch of beastliness, that swollen parcel of dropsies, that huge bombard of sack, that stuffed cloak-bag of guts, that roasted Manningtree ox with the pudding in his belly, that reverend Vice, that grey Iniquity, that father Ruffian, that Vanity in Years? Wherein is he good, but to taste sack and drink it? Wherein neat and cleanly, but to carve a capon and eat it? Wherein cunning, but in craft? Wherein crafty, but in villainy? Wherein villainous, but in all things? Wherein worthy, but in nothing?

FALSTAFF: I would your grace would take me with you. Whom means your grace?

PRINCE HARRY: That villainous, abominable misleader of youth, Falstaff; that old white-bearded Satan.

FALSTAFF: My lord, the man I know.

PRINCE HARRY: I know thou dost.

FALSTAFF: But to say I know more harm in him than in myself were to say more than I know. That he is old, the more the pity, his white hairs do witness it. But that he is, saving your reverence, a whoremaster, that I utterly deny. If sack and sugar be a fault, God help the wicked. If to be old and merry be a sin, then many an old host that I know is damned. If to be fat be to be hated, then Pharaoh's lean kine are to be loved. No, my good lord, banish Peto, banish Bardolph, banish Poins, but for sweet Jack Falstaff, kind Jack Falstaff, true Jack Falstaff, valiant Jack Falstaff, and therefore more valiant, being, as he is, old Jack Falstaff,

Banish not him thy Harry's company,

Banish not him thy Harry's company.

Banish plump Jack, and banish all the world.

PRINCE HARRY: I do; I will.

****

from **Much Ado About Nothing** (1598)

from Act Five Scene Two

CHARACTERS

Benedick
Beatrice
Ursula

[As Benedick waits for Beatrice, he laments that he cannot express his love in poetry. When she arrives, he tells her that he has challenged Claudio to a duel, as she has asked him to do. The two, however, are in love with each other, in spite of themselves, and the banter quickly turns to flirting. Ursula, the maid, enters with news that all the complications of the play have been, or are about to be, resolved.]

BENEDICK: (*Sings.*) The god of love,
That sits above,
And knows me, and knows me,
How pitiful I deserve —
I mean in singing; but in loving, Leander the good swimmer, Troilus the first employer of panders, and a whole book full of these quondam carpet-mongers whose names yet run smoothly in the even road of a blank verse, why they were never so truly turned over and over as my poor self in love. Marry, I cannot show it in rhyme. I have tried: I can find out no rhyme to 'lady' but 'baby', an innocent rhyme; for 'scorn' 'horn', a hard rhyme; for 'school' 'fool', a babbling rhyme. Very ominous endings. No, I was not born under a rhyming planet, nor I cannot woo in festival terms.

(Enter Beatrice.)

Sweet Beatrice, wouldst thou come when I called thee?
BEATRICE: Yea, signior, and depart when you bid me.

BENEDICK: O, stay but till then.

BEATRICE: 'Then' is spoken. Fare you well now. And yet ere I go, let me go with that I came for, which is with knowing what hath passed between you and Claudio.

BENEDICK: Only foul words, and thereupon I will kiss thee.

BEATRICE: Foul words is but foul wind, and foul wind is but foul breath, and foul breath is noisome, therefore I will depart unkissed.

BENEDICK: Thou hast frighted the word out of his right sense, so forcible is thy wit. But I must tell thee plainly, Claudio undergoes my challenge, and either I must shortly hear from him or I will subscribe him a coward. And I pray thee now tell me, for which of my bad parts didst thou first fall in love with me?

BEATRICE: For them all together, which maintain so politic a state of evil that they will not admit any good part to intermingle with them. But for which of my good parts did you first suffer love for me?

BENEDICK: Suffer love — a good epithet. I do suffer love indeed, for I love thee against my will.

BEATRICE: In spite of your heart, I think. Alas, poor heart. If you spite it for my sake I will spite it for yours, for I will never love that which my friend hates.

BENEDICK: Thou and I are too wise to woo peaceably.

BEATRICE: It appears not in this confession. There's not one wise man among twenty that will praise himself.

BENEDICK: An old, an old instance, Beatrice, that lived in the time of good neighbours. If a man do not erect in this age his own tomb ere he dies, he shall live no longer in monument than the bell rings and the widow weeps.

BEATRICE: And how long is that, think you?

BENEDICK: Question — why, an hour in clamour and a quarter in rheum. Therefore is it most expedient for the wise, if Don Worm — his conscience — find no impediment to the contrary, to be the trumpet of his own virtues, as I am to myself. So much for praising myself who, I myself will bear witness, is praiseworthy. And now tell me, how doth your cousin?

BEATRICE: Very ill.

BENEDICK: And how do you?

BEATRICE: Very ill too.

BENEDICK: Serve God, love me, and mend. There will I leave you too, for here comes one in haste.

(Enter Ursula.)

URSULA: Madam, you must come to your uncle. Yonder's old coil at home. It is proved my Lady Hero hath been falsely accused, the Prince and Claudio mightily abused, and Don John is the author of all, who is fled and gone. Will you come presently?

BEATRICE: Will you go hear this news, signior?

BENEDICK: I will live in thy heart, die in thy lap, and be buried in thy eyes. And moreover, I will go with thee to thy uncle's.

(Exeunt.)

****

from **As You Like It** (1599–1600)
from Act Two Scene Seven

[The banished Duke Senior lives with his followers in the Forest of Arden. Among them is the melancholic Jaques. When they encounter the young Orlando and the ancient Adam, who cannot walk due to hunger, they comment on the drama of human life.]

CHARACTERS

Duke Senior

Jaques

DUKE SENIOR: Thou seest we are not all alone unhappy.
This wide and universal theatre
Presents more woeful pageants than the scene
Wherein we play in.
JAQUES: All the world's a stage,
And all the men and women merely players.
They have their exits and their entrances,
And one man in his time plays many parts,
His acts being seven ages. At first the infant,
Mewling and puking in the nurse's arms.
And then the whining schoolboy, with his satchel
And shining morning face, creeping like snail
Unwillingly to school. And then the lover,
Sighing like furnace, with a woeful ballad
Made to his mistress' eyebrow. Then, a soldier,
Full of strange oaths, and bearded like the pard,
Jealous in honour, sudden, and quick in quarrel,
Seeking the bubble reputation
Even in the cannon's mouth. And then the justice,

In fair round belly with good capon lined,
With eyes severe and beard of formal cut,
Full of wise saws and modern instances;
And so he plays his part. The sixth age shifts
Into the lean and slippered pantaloon,
With spectacles on nose and pouch on side,
His youthful hose, well saved, a world too wide
For his shrunk shank, and his big, manly voice,
Turning again toward childish treble, pipes
And whistles in his sound. Last scene of all,
That ends this strange, eventful history,
Is second childishness and mere oblivion,
Sans teeth, sans eyes, sans taste, sans everything.

****

from **Twelfth Night** (1600–1601)

from Act One Scene Five

CHARACTERS

Viola

Olivia

[Viola, disguised as the boy Cesario, has been sent by Duke Orsino to bring messages of love to Countess Olivia. Olivia, tired of Orsino and his servants, plays a trick on Viola by veiling her face and refusing to identify herself. Finally, Olivia dismisses everyone and is left alone with the attractive young messenger, who strays from his/her memorized speech, switches from prose to poetry, and delivers an impressive expression of love. As if hit by lightning, Olivia falls in love.]

OLIVIA: Now, sir, what is your text?

VIOLA: Most sweet lady —

OLIVIA: A comfortable doctrine, and much may be said of it. Where lies your text?

VIOLA: In Orsino's bosom.

OLIVIA: In his bosom? In what chapter of his bosom?

VIOLA: To answer by the method, in the first of his heart.

OLIVIA: O, I have read it. It is heresy. Have you no more to say?

VIOLA: Good madam, let me see your face.

OLIVIA: Have you any commission from your lord to negotiate with my face? You are now out of your text. But we will draw the curtain and show you the picture.

(She unveils.)

Look you, sir, such a one I was this present. Is't not well done?

VIOLA: Excellently done, if God did all.

OLIVIA: 'Tis in grain, sir, 'twill endure wind and weather.

VIOLA: 'Tis beauty truly blent, whose red and white
　　　　Nature's own sweet and cunning hand laid on.
　　　　Lady, you are the cruell'st she alive
　　　　If you will lead these graces to the grave
　　　　And leave the world no copy.
OLIVIA: O sir, I will not be so hard-hearted. I will give out divers sched-
　　　　ules of my beauty. It shall be inventoried, and every particle and
　　　　utensil labelled to my will, as, item, two lips, indifferent red; item,
　　　　two grey eyes, with lids to them; item, one neck, one chin, and so
　　　　forth. Were you sent hither to praise me?
VIOLA: I see you what you are, you are too proud,
　　　　But if you were the devil, you are fair.
　　　　My lord and master loves you. O, such love
　　　　Could be but recompensed though you were crowned
　　　　The nonpareil of beauty.
OLIVIA:　　　　　　　　　　How does he love me?
VIOLA: With adorations, fertile tears,
　　　　With groans that thunder love, with sighs of fire.
OLIVIA: Your lord does know my mind, I cannot love him.
　　　　Yet I suppose him virtuous, know him noble,
　　　　Of great estate, of fresh and stainless youth,
　　　　In voices well divulged, free, learned and valiant,
　　　　And in dimension and the shape of nature
　　　　A gracious person; but yet I cannot love him.
　　　　He might have took his answer long ago.
VIOLA: If I did love you in my master's flame,
　　　　With such a suff'ring, such a deadly life,
　　　　In your denial I would find no sense,
　　　　I would not understand it.
OLIVIA:　　　　　　　　　　Why, what would you?
VIOLA: Make me a willow cabin at your gate
　　　　And call upon my soul within the house,
　　　　Write loyal cantons of contemnèd love,

And sing them loud even in the dead of night;
Halloo your name to the reverberate hills,
And make the babbling gossip of the air
Cry out 'Olivia!' O, you should not rest
Between the elements of air and earth
But you should pity me.

OLIVIA: You might do much.
What is your parentage?

VIOLA: Above my fortunes, yet my state is well.
I am a gentleman.

OLIVIA: Get you to your lord.
I cannot love him. Let him send no more,
Unless, perchance, you come to me again
To tell me how he takes it. Fare you well.
I thank you for your pains. (*Offering a purse.*) Spend this for me.

VIOLA: I am no fee'd post, lady. Keep your purse.
My master, not myself, lacks recompense.
Love make his heart of flint that you shall love,
And let your fervor, like my master's, be
Placed in contempt. Farewell, fair cruelty.

(*Exit.*)

OLIVIA: 'What is your parentage?'
'Above my fortunes, yet my state is well.
I am a gentleman.' I'll be sworn thou art.
Thy tongue, thy face, thy limbs, actions and spirit
Do give thee five-fold blazon. Not too fast. Soft, soft —
Unless the master were the man. How now?
Even so quickly may one catch the plague?
Methinks I feel this youth's perfections
With an invisible and subtle stealth
To creep in at mine eyes. Well, let it be.

****

from **Othello** (1603–1604)

from Act Three Scene Two

CHARACTERS

Othello
Iago
Desdemona
Emilia

[After a drunken brawl, Michael Cassio loses his place as an officer to Othello. He tries to regain the trust of his old friend and general by appealing to Desdemona, Othello's wife. In the span of this short scene, the malevolent Iago, who is jealous of Cassio and contemptuous of Othello, poisons Othello's thoughts with the false notion that Desdemona has been unfaithful with Cassio, setting the drama on its catastrophic course.]

OTHELLO: Was not that Cassio parted from my wife?
IAGO: Cassio, my lord? No, sure, I cannot think it,
    That he would steal away so guilty-like,
    Seeing you coming.
OTHELLO: I do believe 'twas he.
DESDEMONA: How now, my lord?
    I have been talking with a suitor here,
    A man that languishes in your displeasure.
OTHELLO: Who is't you mean?
DESDEMONA: Why, your lieutenant, Cassio; Good my lord,
    If I have any grace or power to move you,
    His present reconciliation take;
    For if he be not one that truly loves you,
    That errs in ignorance and not in cunning,
    I have no judgment in an honest face.

I prithee, call him back.

OTHELLO: Went he hence now?

DESDEMONA: Yes, faith, so humbled
    That he hath left part of his grief with me
    To suffer with him. Good love, call him back.

OTHELLO: Not now, sweet Desdemon. Some other time.

DESDEMONA: But shall't be shortly?

OTHELLO: The sooner, sweet, for you.

DESDEMONA: Shall't be to-night at supper?

OTHELLO: No, not tonight.

DESDEMONA: Tomorrow dinner, then?

OTHELLO: I shall not dine at home.
    I meet the captains at the citadel.

DESDEMONA: Why, then, tomorrow night, or Tuesday morn,
    On Tuesday noon, or night, on Wednesday morn —
    I prithee, name the time, but let it not
    Exceed three days. In faith, he's penitent,
    And yet his trespass, in our common reason —
    Save that, they say, the wars must make example
    Out of their best — is not almost a fault
    T'incur a private check. When shall he come?
    Tell me, Othello. I wonder in my soul,
    What you would ask me that I should deny,
    Or stand so mamm'ring on. What, Michael Cassio,
    That came a-wooing with you, and so many a time,
    When I have spoke of you dispraisingly
    Hath ta'en your part — to have so much to-do
    To bring him in? By'r Lady, I could do much.

OTHELLO: Prithee, no more. Let him come when he will.
    I will deny thee nothing.

DESDEMONA: Why, this is not a boon.
    'Tis as I should entreat you wear your gloves,
    Or feed on nourishing dishes, or keep you warm,

Or sue to you to do a peculiar profit

To your own person. Nay, when I have a suit

Wherein I mean to touch your love indeed,

It shall be full of poise and difficult weight,

And fearful to be granted.

OTHELLO: I will deny thee nothing,

Whereon I do beseech thee grant me this:

To leave me but a little to myself.

DESDEMONA: Shall I deny you? No. Farewell, my lord.

OTHELLO: Farewell, my Desdemona. I'll come to thee straight.

DESDEMONA: Emilia, come. (*To Othello.*) Be as your fancies teach you.

Whate'er you be, I am obedient.

(Exeunt Desdemona and Emilia.)

OTHELLO: Excellent wretch! Perdition catch my soul

But I do love thee, and when I love thee not,

Chaos is come again.

IAGO: My noble lord —

OTHELLO: What dost thou say, Iago?

IAGO: Did Michael Cassio, when you wooed my lady,

Know of your love?

OTHELLO: He did, from first to last. Why dost thou ask?

IAGO: But for a satisfaction of my thought,

No further harm.

OTHELLO: Why of thy thought, Iago?

IAGO: I did not think he had been acquainted with her.

OTHELLO: O yes; and went between us very oft.

IAGO: Indeed?

OTHELLO: Indeed? Ay, indeed. Discern'st thou aught in that?

Is he not honest?

IAGO: Honest, my lord?

OTHELLO: Honest? Ay, honest.

IAGO: My lord, for aught I know.

OTHELLO: What dost thou think?

IAGO: Think, my lord?

OTHELLO: 'Think, my lord?' By heaven, he echo'st me
As if there were some monster in his thought
Too hideous to be shown. Thou dost mean something.
I heard thee say even now thou liked'st not that,
When Cassio left my wife. What didst not like?
And when I told thee he was of my counsel
In my whole course of wooing, thou cried'st 'Indeed?'
And didst contract and purse thy brow together
As if thou then hadst shut up in thy brain
Some horrible conceit. If thou dost love me,
Show me thy thought.

IAGO: My lord, you know I love you.

OTHELLO: I think thou dost;
And, for I know thou'rt full of love and honesty,
And weigh'st thy words before thou giv'st them breath,
Therefore these stops of thine fright me the more;
For such things in a false disloyal knave
Are tricks of custom, but in a man that's just,
They are close dilations, working from the heart
That passion cannot rule.

IAGO: For Michael Cassio,
I dare be sworn I think that he is honest.

OTHELLO: I think so too.

IAGO: Men should be what they seem,
Or those that be not, would they might seem none.

OTHELLO: Certain, men should be what they seem.

IAGO: Why then, I think Cassio's an honest man.

OTHELLO: Nay, yet there's more in this.
I prithee speak to me as to thy thinkings,
As thou dost ruminate, and give thy worst of thoughts
The worst of words.

IAGO: Good my lord, pardon me.
  Though I am bound to every act of duty,
  I am not bound to that all slaves are free to.
  Utter my thoughts? Why, say they are vile and false,
  As where's that palace whereinto foul things
  Sometimes intrude not? Who has that breast so pure
  But some uncleanly apprehensions
  Keep leets and law-days and in sessions sit
  With meditations lawful?
OTHELLO: Thou dost conspire against thy friend, Iago,
  If thou but think'st him wronged and mak'st his ear
  A stranger to thy thoughts.
IAGO: I do beseech you,
  Though I perchance am vicious in my guess —
  As, I confess, it is my nature's plague
  To spy into abuses, and oft my jealousy
  Shapes faults that are not — that your wisdom then,
  From one that so imperfectly conceits,
  Would take no notice, nor build yourself a trouble
  Out of his scattering and unsure observance.
  It were not for your quiet nor your good,
  Nor for my manhood, honesty, and wisdom,
  To let you know my thoughts.
OTHELLO: What dost thou mean?
IAGO: Good name in man and woman, dear my lord,
  Is the immediate jewel of their souls.
  Who steals my purse steals trash; 'tis something, nothing;
  'Twas mine, 'tis his, and has been slave to thousands.
  But he that filches from me my good name
  Robs me of that which not enriches him
  And makes me poor indeed.
OTHELLO: By heaven, I'll know thy thoughts.
IAGO: You cannot, if my heart were in your hand;
  Nor shall not whilst 'tis in my custody.

OTHELLO: Ha!

IAGO: O, beware, my lord, of jealousy.

    It is the green-eyed monster which doth mock

    The meat it feeds on. That cuckold lives in bliss

    Who, certain of his fate, loves not his wronger.

    But, O, what damnèd minutes tells he o'er

    Who dotes yet doubts, suspects yet strongly loves!

OTHELLO: O misery!

IAGO: Poor and content is rich and rich enough,

    But riches fineless is as poor as winter

    To him that ever fears he shall be poor.

    Good God the souls of all my tribe defend

    From jealousy!

OTHELLO: Why, why is this?

    Think'st thou I'd make a lie of jealousy,

    To follow still the changes of the moon

    With fresh suspicions? No, to be once in doubt

    Is once to be resolved. Exchange me for a goat

    When I shall turn the business of my soul

    To such exsufflicate and blown surmises

    Matching thy inference. 'Tis not to make me jealous

    To say my wife is fair, feeds well, loves company,

    Is free of speech, sings, plays and dances well.

    Where virtue is, these are more virtuous,

    Nor from mine own weak merits will I draw

    The smallest fear or doubt of her revolt,

    For she had eyes and chose me. No, Iago,

    I'll see before I doubt; when I doubt, prove;

    And on the proof, there is no more but this:

    Away at once with love or jealousy.

IAGO: I am glad of this, for now I shall have reason

    To show the love and duty that I bear you

    With franker spirit. Therefore, as I am bound,

Receive it from me. I speak not yet of proof.
Look to your wife. Observe her well with Cassio.
Wear your eye thus: not jealous, nor secure.
I would not have your free and noble nature,
Out of self-bounty be abused. Look to't.
I know our country disposition well.
In Venice they do let God see the pranks
They dare not show their husbands; their best conscience
Is not to leave't undone, but keep't unknown.

OTHELLO: Dost thou say so?

IAGO: She did deceive her father, marrying you,
And when she seem'd to shake and fear your looks
She loved them most.

OTHELLO: And so she did.

IAGO: Why, go to, then.
She that so young, could give out such a seeming,
To seel her father's eyes up close as oak —
He thought 'twas witchcraft! But I am much to blame.
I humbly do beseech you of your pardon
For too much loving you.

OTHELLO: I am bound to thee for ever.

IAGO: I see this hath a little dash'd your spirits.

OTHELLO: Not a jot, not a jot.

IAGO: I'faith, I fear it has.
I hope you will consider what is spoke
Comes from my love. But I do see you're moved.
I am to pray you not to strain my speech
To grosser issues, nor to larger reach
Than to suspicion.

OTHELLO: I will not.

IAGO: Should you do so, my lord,
My speech should fall into such vile success
Which my thoughts aimed not at. Cassio's my worthy friend.
My lord, I see you're moved.

OTHELLO: No, not much moved.

    I do not think but Desdemona's honest.

IAGO: Long live she so, and long live you to think so!

OTHELLO: And yet how nature, erring from itself —

IAGO: Ay, there's the point; as, to be bold with you,

    Not to affect many proposèd matches

    Of her own clime, complexion, and degree,

    Whereto we see in all things nature tends.

    Foh, one may smell in such a will most rank,

    Foul disproportions, thoughts unnatural!

    But pardon me. I do not in position

    Distinctly speak of her, though I may fear

    Her will, recoiling to her better judgment,

    May fall to match you with her country forms

    And happily repent.

OTHELLO: Farewell, farewell.

    If more thou dost perceive, let me know more.

    Set on thy wife to observe. Leave me, Iago.

IAGO: (*Going.*) My lord, I take my leave.

OTHELLO: Why did I marry? This honest creature doubtless

    Sees and knows more, much more, than he unfolds.

IAGO: (*Returning.*) My lord, I would I might entreat your honour

    To scan this thing no farther. Leave it to time.

    Although 'tis fit that Cassio have his place —

    For sure he fills it up with great ability —

    Yet, if you please to hold him off awhile,

    You shall by that perceive him and his means.

    Note if your lady strain his entertainment

    With any strong or vehement importunity.

    Much will be seen in that. In the mean time,

    Let me be thought too busy in my fears —

    As worthy cause I have to fear I am —

    And hold her free, I do beseech your honour.

OTHELLO: Fear not my government.

IAGO: I once more take my leave.

(Exit.)

OTHELLO: This fellow's of exceeding honesty,
    And knows all qualities, with a learned spirit
    Of human dealings. If I do prove her haggard,
    Though that her jesses were my dear heart-strings,
    I'd whistle her off and let her down the wind
    To pray at fortune. Haply for I am black,
    And have not those soft parts of conversation
    That chamberers have; or for I am declined
    Into the vale of years — yet thats not much —
    She's gone. I am abused, and my relief
    Must be to loathe her. O curse of marriage,
    That we can call these delicate creatures ours,
    And not their appetites! I had rather be a toad
    And live upon the vapour of a dungeon
    Than keep a corner in the thing I love
    For others' uses. Yet, 'tis the plague of great ones;
    Prerogatived are they less than the base.
    'Tis destiny unshunnable, like death.
    Even then this forkèd plague is fated to us
    When we do quicken.

(Enter Desdemona and Emilia.)

                Look, where she comes.
    If she be false, O then heaven mocks itself!
    I'll not believe't.

DESDEMONA: How now, my dear Othello?
    Your dinner, and the generous islanders
    By you invited, do attend your presence.

OTHELLO: I am to blame.

DESDEMONA: Why do you speak so faintly? Are you not well?

OTHELLO: I have a pain upon my forehead here.

DESDEMONA: Faith, that's with watching. 'Twill away again.

Let me but bind it hard, within this hour

It will be well.

OTHELLO: Your napkin is too little:

(He puts the handkerchief from him. It drops.)

Let it alone. Come, I'll go in with you.

DESDEMONA: I am very sorry that you are not well.

(Exeunt Othello and Desdemona.)

****

from **Antony and Cleopatra** (1606)

from Act Five Scene Two

CHARACTERS

Cleopatra

Dolabella

[Cleopatra is a prisoner of Octavius Caesar, fearing that she will be paraded though the streets as a captive. In this exchange between Cleopatra and Dolabella, one of Octavius Caesar's men sent to guard the queen, Cleopatra recounts a vision in which she saw her dead lover Antony as a god-like hero.]

CLEOPATRA: I dreamt there was an Emperor Antony.
    O, such another sleep, that I might see
    But such another man!
DOLABELLA: If it might please ye —
CLEOPATRA: His face was as the heav'ns, and therein stuck
    A sun and moon, which kept their course, and lighted
    The little O, o'th' earth.
DOLABELLA: Most sovereign creature —
CLEOPATRA: His legs bestrid the ocean; his reared arm
    Crested the world. His voice was propertied
    As all the tunèd spheres, and that to friends;
    But when he meant to quail and shake the orb,
    He was as rattling thunder. For his bounty,
    There was no winter in't; an autumn 'twas,
    That grew the more by reaping. His delights
    Were dolphin-like; they showed his back above
    The element they lived in. In his livery
    Walked crowns and crownets. Realms and islands were
    As plates dropped from his pocket.

DOLABELLA: Cleopatra —

CLEOPATRA: Think you there was, or might be, such a man

    As this I dreamt of?

DOLABELLA: Gentle madam, no.

CLEOPATRA: You lie, up to the hearing of the gods.

    But, if there be, or ever were one such,

    It's past the size of dreaming. Nature wants stuff

    To vie strange forms with fancy; yet, t'imagine

    An Antony, were nature's piece 'gainst fancy,

    Condemning shadows quite.

****

THE READING ROOM

YOUNG ACTORS AND THEIR TEACHERS

Ackroyd, Peter. *Shakespeare: The Biography*. New York: Nan A. Talese/Doubleday, 2005.

Barnet, Sylvan. *A Short Guide to Shakespeare*. New York: Harcourt Brace Jovanovitch, 1974.

Bate, Jonathan. *The Genius of Shakespeare*. London: Picador, 1977.

Beard, Jocelyn, ed. *100 Great Monologues from the Renaissance Theater*. Lyme, N.H.: Smith and Kraus, 1994.

Bentley, Gerald E. *Shakespeare's Life: A Biographical Handbook*. New Haven, Conn.: Yale University Press, 1961.

Brine, Adrian and Michael York. *A Shakespearian Actor Prepares*. Lyme, N.H.: Smith and Kraus, 2000.

Burgess, Anthony. *Shakespeare*. London: Jonathan Cape, 1970.

Chute, Marchette. *Shakespeare of London*. New York: E. P. Dutton, 1949.

Clark, Cumberland. *The Eternal Shakespeare*. London: Williams & Norgate, 1930.

Cohen, Robert. *Acting in Shakespeare*. Lyme, N.H.: Smith and Kraus, 2005.

Duncan-Jones, Katherine. *Ungentle Shakespeare: Scenes from His Life*. London: Arden Shakespeare, 2001.

Fox, Levi, ed. *The Shakespeare Handbook*. Boston: Hall, 1987.

Fraser, Russell A. *Young Shakespeare*. New York: Columbia University Press, 1988.

Frye, Roland Mushat. *Shakespeare's Life and Times: A Pictorial Record*. Princeton, N.J.: Princeton University Press, 1967.

Harrison, G. B. *Introducing Shakespeare*. 3rd ed. London: Penguin Books, 1991.

This extensive bibliography lists books about the playwright according to whom the books might be of interest. If you would like to research further something that interests you in the text, lists of references, sources cited, and editions used in this book are found in this section.

Holden, Anthony. *William Shakespeare: The Man Behind the Genius.* Boston: Little, Brown, 1999.

Honan, Park. *Shakespeare: A Life.* Oxford, New York: Oxford University Press, 1998.

Hyland, Peter. *An Introduction to Shakespeare: The Dramatist in His Context.* Basingstoke, Hampshire: Macmillan, 1996.

Levi, Peter. *The Life and Times of William Shakespeare.* London: Macmillan, 1988.

Lloyd Evans, Gareth, and Barbara. *The Shakespeare Companion.* New York: Scribners, 1978.

Olster, Fredi and Rick Hamilton. *Discovering Shakespeare: A Midsummer Night's Dream: A Workbook for Students.* Lyme, N.H.: Smith and Kraus, 1996.

_____. *Discovering Shakespeare: Romeo and Juliet: A Workbook for Students.* Lyme, N.H.: Smith and Kraus, 1996.

_____. *Discovering Shakespeare: The Taming of the Shrew: A Workbook for Students.* Lyme, N.H.: Smith and Kraus, 1997.

_____. *Discovering Shakespeare: Much Ado About Nothing: A Workbook for Students.* Lyme, N.H.: Smith and Kraus, 1998.

_____. *Discovering Shakespeare: Macbeth: A Workbook for Students.* Lyme, N.H.: Smith and Kraus, 2000.

_____. *Shakespeare Alive! 2-Minute Speeches and Monologues for Study, Audition, and Performance.* Lyme, N.H.: Smith and Kraus, 2004.

Quennell, Peter. *Shakespeare, the Poet and His Background.* London: Weidenfeld and Nicolson, 1963.

Reese, M. M. *Shakespeare: His World and His Work.* London: Edward Arnold, 1953.

Saccio, Peter. *Shakespeare's English Kings.* 2nd ed. New York: Oxford University Press, 2000.

Scheeder, Louis and Shane Ann Younts. *All the Words on Stage: A Complete Pronunciation Dictionary for the Plays of William Shakespeare.* Lyme, N.H.: Smith and Kraus, 2002.

Somerset, Anne. *Elizabeth I.* New York: Alfred A. Knopf, 1992.

Speaight, Robert. *Shakespeare, the Man and His Achievement.* London: J. M. Dent, 1977.

Timmerman, Diane. *90-Minute Theater: A Midsummer Night's Dream.* Lyme, N.H.: Smith and Kraus, 2001.

_____. *90-Minute Theater: Romeo and Juliet.* Lyme, N.H.: Smith and Kraus, 2001.

Weinstein, Elizabeth. *Shakespeare with Children: Six Scripts for Young Players.* Lyme, N.H.: Smith and Kraus, 2008.

Wood, Michael. *In Search of Shakespeare.* London: BBC, 2003.

SCHOLARS, STUDENTS, PROFESSORS

Baker, Oliver. *In Shakespeare's Warwickshire and the Unknown Years.* London: S. Marshall, 1937.

Barroll, J. Leeds. *Politics, Plague, and Shakespeare's Theater: The Stuart Years.* Ithaca, N.Y.: Cornell University Press, 1991.

Cavell, Stanley. *Disowning Knowledge in Six Plays of Shakespeare.* Cambridge: Cambridge University Play, 1987.

Cohen, Derek. *Shakespeare's Culture of Violence.* London: Macmillan, 1993.

Calderwood, James. *Shakespeare and the Denial of Death.* Amherst, Mass.: University of Massachusetts Press, 1987.

de Grazia, Margreta, and Stanley Wells, eds. *The Cambridge Companion to Shakespeare.* Cambridge: Cambridge University Press, 2001.

Dollimore, Jonathan. *Radical Tragedy.* Chicago: University of Chicago Press, 1984.

_____ and Alan Sinfield, eds. *Political Shakespeare: New Essays in Cultural Materialism.* Ithaca, N.Y.: Cornell University Press, 1985.

Drakakis, John, ed. *Alternative Shakespeares.* London: Methuen, 1985.

Frye, Northrop. *A Natural Perspective: The Development of Shakespearean Comedy and Romance.* San Diego: Harcourt, Brace, Jovanovich, 1965.

_____. *Northrop Frye on Shakespeare.* Ed. by Robert Sandler. New Haven, Conn.: Yale University Press, 1986.

Honigmann, E. A. J. *Shakespeare: The "Lost Years."* Manchester: Manchester University Press, 1985.

Garber, Marjorie. *Shakespeare After All.* New York: Pantheon, 2004.

Hotson, Leslie. *Mr. W. H.* London: Rupert Hart-Davis, 1964.

Hunt, Margaret R. *The Middling Sort: Commerce, Gender, and the Family in England, 1680–1780.* Berkeley: University of California Press, 1996.

Kahn, Coppelia. *Man's Estate: Masculine Identity in Shakespeare.* Berkeley: University of California Press, 1981.

Kaston, David Scott. *Shakespeare After Theory*. New York: Routledge, 1999.

Kernan, Alvin B., ed. *Modern Shakespearean Criticism*. San Francisco: Harcourt, Brace, and World, 1970.

Knight, William Nicholas. *Shakespeare's Hidden Life: Shakespeare at the Law, 1585–1595*. New York: Mason & Lipscomb, 1973.

Lewis, B. Roland. *The Shakespeare Documents, Facsimiles, Translitera-tions, Translations & Commentary*, 2 vols. Stanford: Stanford University Press, 1940.

Matus, Irvin Leigh. *Shakespeare: The Living Record*. New York: St. Martin's Press, 1991.

McDonald, Russ. *Shakespeare & Jonson, Jonson & Shakespeare*. Lincoln: University of Nebraska Press, 1988.

Muir, Kenneth. *Shakespeare's Sources*. London: Methuen, 1957.

Nuttall, A. D. *Shakespeare the Thinker*. New Haven, Conn.: Yale University Press, 2007.

Plimpton, George Arthur. *The Education of Shakespeare Illustrated from the Schoolbooks in Use in His Time*. London, New York: Oxford University Press, 1933.

Sams, Eric. *The Real Shakespeare: Retrieving the Early Years, 1564–1594*. New Haven, Conn.: Yale University Press, 1995.

Schmidgall, Gary. *Shakespeare and the Poet's Life*. Lexington: University Press of Kentucky, 1990.

Schoenbaum, S. *Shakespeare's Lives*. New York: Oxford University Press, 1970.

_____. *William Shakespeare: A Documentary Life*. New York: Oxford University Press, 1975.

_____. *William Shakespeare: Records and Images*. New York: Oxford University Press, 1981.

Thorndike, Arthur Russell. *In the Steps of Shakespeare*. London, New York: Rich and Cowan, 1948.

Vickers, Brian. *Shakespeare: The Critical Heritage*. 6 vols. London: Routledge and K. Paul, 1974–81.

THEATER, PRODUCERS

Aubrey, John. *Brief Lives: A Selection Based on Existing Contemporary Portraits*. Ed. by Richard Barber. London: The Folio Society, 1975.

Greenblatt, Stephen. *Will in the World.* New York: W. W. Norton, 2004.

Mingay, George E.. *The Gentry: The Rise and Fall of a Ruling Class.* London: Longman, 1976.

Partridge, Eric. *Shakespeare's Bawdy.* Revised ed. London: Routledge and Kegan Paul, 1955.

Seccombe, Thomas and J.W. Allen. *The Age of Shakespeare (1579–1631).* 2 vols. London: G. Bell, 1903.

Shapiro, James. *A Year in the Life of William Shakespeare: 1599.* New York: HarperCollins, 2005.

Sheavyn, Phoebe Anne. *The Literature Profession in the Elizabethan Age.* 2nd ed. Manchester: Manchester University Press, 1967.

Southworth, John. *Shakespeare, the Player: A Life in the Theatre.* Stroud, Gloucestershire: Sutton, 2000.

Thompson, Peter. *Shakespeare's Professional Career.* Cambridge: Cambridge University Press, 1992.

ACTORS, DIRECTORS, THEATER PROFESSIONALS

Barber, C. L. *Shakespeare's Festive Comedy.* Princeton, N.J.: Princeton University Press, 1959.

Bate, Jonathan, and Russell Jackson. *Shakespeare: An Illustrated Stage History.* Oxford: Oxford University Press, 1996.

Bryson, Bill. *Shakespeare: The World as Stage.* New York: HarperCollins, 2007.

Bullough, Geoffrey. *Narrative and Dramatic Sources of Shakespeare.* New York: Columbia University Press, 1957–75.

Chambers, E.K. *The Medieval Stage.* 2 vols. London: Oxford University Press, 1903.

——————. *The Elizabethan Stage.* 4 vols. Oxford: Clarendon Press, 1951.

Gurr, Andrew. *Playgoing in Shakespeare's London.* 2nd ed. Cambridge: Cambridge University Press, 1996.

Gurr, Andrew, and Ichikawa Mariko. *Staging in Shakespeare's Theatres.* Oxford: Oxford University Press, 2000.

Halliday, F. E. *Shakespeare: A Pictorial Biography.* London: Clarke and Sherwell Ltd., 1956.

——————. *A Shakespeare Companion, 1564–1964.* Harmondsworth: Penguin Books, 1964.

Hattaway, Michael. *Elizabethan Popular Theatre: Plays in Performance*. London: Routledge & Kegan Paul, 1982.

Honigmann, E. A. J. and Susan Brock, eds. *Playhouse Wills 1558–1642: An Edition of Wills by Shakespeare and His Contemporaries in the London Theatre*. Manchester: Manchester University Press, 1993.

Kermode, Frank. *Shakespeare's Language*. New York: Penguin, 2000.

_____. *The Age of Shakespeare*. New York: Modern Library, 2004.

Parsons, Keith and Pamela Mason, eds. *Shakespeare in Performance*. London: Salamander Books Ltd, 1995.

Raleigh, Walter Alexander, Sidney Lee, and C. T. Onions. *Shakespeare's England; an Account of the Life and Manners of His Age*. 2 vols. Oxford: Clarendon Press, 1916.

Schoenbaum, S. *William Shakespeare: A Compact Documentary Life*. New York: Oxford University Press, 1977.

Styan, J. L. *Shakespeare's Stagecraft*. Cambridge: Cambridge University Press, 1971.

Wells, Stanley W. *Shakespeare, a Dramatic Life*. London: Sinclair-Stevenson, 1994.

_____. *A Dictionary of Shakespeare*. Oxford: Oxford University Press, 1998.

Wells, Stanley W. and Gary Taylor. *William Shakespeare: A Textual Companion*. Oxford: Oxford University Press, 1987.

THE EDITIONS OF SHAKESPEARE'S WORKS USED FOR THIS BOOK

The Arden Shakespeare Complete Works. Ed. by Richard Proudfoot, Ann Thompson, and David Scott Kastan. London: Arden Shakespeare/Thompson Learning, 2001, 2007.

The Complete Oxford Shakespeare. Ed. by Stanley Wells, Gary Taylor, John Jowett, and William Montgomery. Oxford: Oxford University Press, 1987.

SOURCES CITED IN THIS BOOK

Bloom, Harold. *Shakespeare: The Invention of the Human*. New York: Riverhead, 1998.

Greene, Robert. *Groats-Worth of Witte, Bought with a Million of Repentance. The Repentance of Robert Greene, 1592.* Edinburgh: Edinburgh University Press, 1966.

Meres, Francis. *Palladis Tamia.* New York: Scholars' Facsimiles & Reprints, 2000.

Wilson, J. Dover. *The Essential Shakespeare: A Biographical Adventure.* Cambridge: Cambridge University Press, 1932.

WEB SITES

Royal Shakespeare Company: www.rsc.org

Shakespeare Birthplace Trust: www.shakespeare.org.uk

Shakespeare's Globe: www.shakespeares-globe.org

The Shakespeare Theatre (Washington, D.C.): www.shakespeare.org

INDEX

ABOUT THE AUTHOR

Christopher Baker is senior dramaturg at Hartford Stage, where he has been since 1998, and a visiting lecturer at the University of Massachusetts. He previously served as the dramaturg for The Shakespeare Theatre, PlayMakers Repertory Company, and the Alley Theatre and taught at the University of North Carolina and the Hartt School. As a director he has staged many works, including his own play for children, *Calliope Jam*. A contributor to the book *The Production Notebooks*, his articles have appeared in *Theatre Journal*, *Hog River Journal*, *American Theatre* magazine, the *Hartford Courant*, and the book *The Lively ART*.

Know the playwright, love the play.

Open a new door to theater study, performance, and audience satisfaction with these Playwrights In an Hour titles.

ANCIENT GREEK

Aeschylus   Aristophanes   Euripides   Sophocles

RENAISSANCE

William Shakespeare

MODERN

Anton Chekhov   Noël Coward   Lorraine Hansberry
Henrik Ibsen   Arthur Miller   Molière   Eugene O'Neill
Arthur Schnitzler   George Bernard Shaw   August Strindberg
Frank Wedekind   Oscar Wilde   Thornton Wilder
Tennessee Williams

CONTEMPORARY

Edward Albee   Alan Ayckbourn   Samuel Beckett
Theresa Rebeck   Sarah Ruhl   Sam Shepard   Tom Stoppard
August Wilson

To purchase or for more information
visit our web site inanhourbooks.com